The Sporting Minis

The Sporting Minis
Mini-Cooper, Mini-Cooper S, 1275GT

A collector's guide
by John Brigden

Thirty years old it may have been in the summer of 1989, but the Mini-Cooper was still enjoying an active competition career. These were two of the cars which competed in the second Pirelli Classic Marathon and were on display a few days later at the Bromley Pageant of Motoring in Kent.

An early Mini-Cooper S, complete with brake servo. The 16-bladed fan, which greatly improved engine cooling, is another distinguishing feature, while the air filter cover and the twin SU carburettors are further identification points of this most desirable of Minis.

Introduction

The Mini is one of the world's great survivors, having now been in production for 30 years. When it was first launched there weren't many people who would have given you odds that it would have survived 10 years, let alone as long as it has.

Its longevity is as much a testament to its creator and designer Alec Issigonis as to the manufacturer that has continued to respond to the public demand for such an individual little car. Had it been produced by any other company there is little doubt that this car would not still be with us today.

This is all the more remarkable when one considers that for most of its existence it has been shown not to make a profit – or much of a profit at the best of times.

Car design and engineering developments have left the Mini far behind but because of its individuality it is still as popular as ever. With cars designed by committees, marketing men and wind tunnels these days, the Mini stands out as a beacon for the triumph of vision over common sense – and thank God for that.

What of the future of the Mini? It has been gradually emasculated until it is just a two-model range with a few special editions thrown in to keep the interest going, but in reality I doubt if we will be celebrating its 40th anniversary of continuous production.

However, the prediction game is one in which I claim no special abilities. It always reminds me of a comment from my father when, as an eight-year-old boy, I expressed my wish to be old enough to drive. He replied by saying that by the time I was old enough to drive, cars would be obsolete and we would have some other means of transport. That was in the year the Mini was launched!

In this book I have attempted to do justice to the different elements which have gone into making the Mini legend. These include the design, technical innovations, sporting achievements and model range. Regarding production details, there are some discrepancies, according to whom you listen to, so I have taken the official figures. When it comes to tuning the Mini, there is also more than my way of doing it, but the details here reflect the traditional methods – methods which most tuners will use, be they professionals or amateurs.

As a Mini owner and racer, I hope that through these pages I have managed to convey some of my enthusiasm for the car and its creators.

September 1989   JOHN BRIGDEN

Acknowledgements

Where do you start? Over the years I have probably talked more about Minis than any other single vehicle to more people in more places than I care to remember. All of these have contributed something to this book. But to avoid a long list I will start with those whose input was quite direct.

I am indebted to Dr Alex Moulton, who gave our mutual friend Ronald Barker and myself a highly entertaining day, full of interesting insights into not only Issigonis but the period during which the car was developed. His own work can still be seen in the Metro suspension.

I should like to thank Ron Unsworth, who was in Issigonis' team building the Morris Minor and who helped with verifying some of the information. Jan Odor of Janspeed has contributed, not only to the book, but also to my enjoyment of the motoring world in general and is without doubt one of the gentlemen of the tuning world.

Those who have assisted greatly include Roger Tolliday, who oversaw the preparation of my Mini racer and my mechanical education at the same time. Perhaps I should also mention Gordon Davidson and Rob Lancaster-Gaye, who needed another mug to help them buy a racing car, but both dropped out leaving me to run the car.

Then there were the inspirations from such as David Enderby, Peter Baldwin and Peter Day. And of course I must mention Paul Davies and Terry Grimwood, who indulged me at *Cars and Car Conversions*.

And finally, no acknowledgement concerning the Mini would be complete without mentioning the late Sir Alec Issigonis whose vision and single-mindedness produced one of the great cars of history.

CHAPTER 1

The right car, the right time

Origins of the Mini phenomenon

The history of motoring is littered with the right cars at the wrong time or the wrong cars at the right time, but there are a very few which you can point to and say, 'the right car at the right time'. The Mini is one.

Not only was it the right car at the right time, but it had two other great advantages; it was also at the right place and at the right price. It came to personify its era – the 1960s.

The Mini was the symbol of the age, providing a vehicle in which people could do almost anything and get away with it. It was a classless and universal car in which Royalty and riff raff could both drive around and feel equally comfortable. The fact that Lord Snowdon and Princess Anne both owned one also gave the Mini the kind of cachet and publicity that would be impossible to buy.

The BMC marketing department could probably hardly believe their luck when the car became a cult and was beginning to get publicity for anything, from being coated with pennies, to squeezing as many people into one as possible. Other bizarre publicity came from such earth-shattering pronouncements as the one handed down by one innocent judge who said that it was impossible to have sex in a Mini.

But it wasn't all court cases and *The Guinness Book of Records.*

It quickly became obvious that the little Mini was capable of mighty things and was soon leading a British revival in motorsport – particularly in rallying, where its amazing roadholding and handling quickly made it *the* car to chase. That the French had to resort to dubious rule interpretation to exclude it from the Monte Carlo Rally in 1966, and let one of their beloved Citroen DSs win, only goes to underline its phenomenal impact.

Despite its exclusion from that Monte Carlo Rally, or maybe because of it, the French have had a love affair with the Mini ever since. They are not the only ones. Ask almost any Continental which car Britain is most famous for and he or she will name the Mini, and many of them will have owned one at some time in their driving careers. Even the Americans had a brief fling with the Mini, but the Big Country proved just a touch too big, and anyway the car was to be legislated out of the showrooms.

Most cars represent a progression in design or functionality and with a bit of thought they can be predicted. There are a select few which represent such large jumps that they are impossible to foresee. Citroen have produced their fair share, the *Traction Avant*, the 2CV, and the DS ranges; VW produced the Beetle; Austin the Austin 7; Morris the Morris Minor; and BMC the Mini.

It is true that Citroen pioneered the full production use of front-wheel drive and Sir Alec Issigonis was always the first to acknowledge the debt, but they were on their own for many years. The Morris Minor was the first all-Issigonis design and was certainly a giant step forward for the postwar era, but it did not have the same impact on the whole motoring world as the diminutive Mini.

That the Mini spawned a whole series of imitators is well chronicled, but just how it came about is perhaps not so well known.

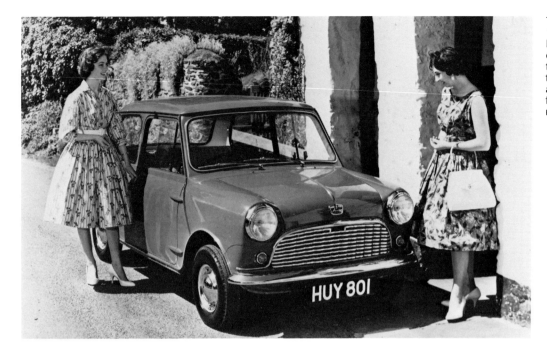

The Mini was introduced in August 1959 as the Austin Seven (and Morris Mini-Minor). This was badge engineering of an extreme sort as the only real differences between the two cars were the name badges and the grille. Note the late-1950s fashion for the young upwardly mobile ladies of the day.

When Issigonis was asked by Leonard Lord to become Chief Engineer at BMC, which had been formed by the merger of Austin and Morris, he had been working for Alvis on a front-wheel-drive car with independent suspension by rubber.

According to legend, Len Lord started the whole Mini car chase with his remark, 'God damn those bloody awful bubble cars. We must drive them off the streets by designing a proper minature car'. No doubt much the same sentiment had been in Herbert Austin's mind when he set about designing the Austin 7 on his billiard table and removing cycle-cars from the roads. He succeeded and, incidentally, along the way may have given a helping hand to Datsun, not to mention BMW, whose first offering was an Austin 7 made under licence. Datsun built a car so similar to the Austin 7 that Herbert Austin imported one to see if he had legal grounds to sue!

The supposed Len Lord statement dates from the time of the Suez Crisis, when he was also quoted as wanting a car to beat petrol rationing.

The facts don't quite support this theory, though, as according to Alex Moulton, Issigonis' close friend and inventor of the Mini suspension, there were a number of projects which Issigonis was working on before Suez and the Mini was just the small car of a range that they had in the pipeline. The car Issigonis was giving most attention to in 1956 when Britain decided on its Egyptian adventure was a 1,500cc family-sized car. It was only after Suez, when Len Lord realized the full impact of the crisis, that attention was switched to the small car.

Of course, BMC wasn't the only company working on small cars; Rootes also saw the scale of the crisis and they set about producing one of their own, the Hillman Imp. They worked quickly, but were left standing by the Issigonis

team. Imagine the dismay at Hillman when they saw their clever new model beaten by a mile to the showrooms. History might have been different if they had succeeded in getting their car out first.

Some versions of history show that the Mini didn't make much money, but it was nothing compared to the losses made by Rootes over the Imp, which are reputed to have been around the £9 million mark – and that was when a pound in your pocket meant just that.

In March 1957, some while after Suez, Leonard Lord took the final decision to stop work on the other Issigonis projects and go all-out for the small car.

Small cars, of course, were a British tradition which had continued gloriously after the war. There was the Austin A30 and A35, which I always thought of as reminiscent of a bomb casing, then there was the A40 which, while looking different from the A35, was based on its running gear. No-one could have seen at that time that the sun was setting on the conventional rear-wheel drive configuration, except one man and his notepad.

Alec Issigonis, knighted in 1969, was above all a brilliant communicator of ideas through his drawings. A man who disliked interference, he produced his best designs when able to work with a small team. Born in Smyrna, Turkey, in 1906, he died in England in 1988.

A 1959 publicity shot for the launch of the Mini. The wickerwork baskets were a custom-designed set for the Mini. The Mini may have been an outstanding example of space utilization, but seven people AND all that baggage? No wonder they aren't smiling.

Issigonis in his Lightweight Special which he built with George Dowson during the 1930s. This picture was taken at Silverstone in the 1960s; standing behind the car in the dark suit is Charles Griffin, BMC Chief Engineer, and George Dowson is on his right.

Issigonis, right, with George Harriman discussing an early Mini. Harriman succeeded Leonard Lord as Chairman and Managing Director of BMC. Although Lord had instigated the Mini project, it was Harriman who gave the nod to build the Mini-Cooper.

The Mini caused great public interest, particularly with the press, who hailed its arrival enthusiastically. The public, however, were initially a little more cautious, believing that the mechanicals looked a trifle difficult to access – as in those days many more people did their own servicing. Designed as the British 'People's Car', it didn't catch on until the likes of Lord Snowdon and The Queen, who was given a demonstration by Issigonis, gave it their seal of approval.

There were problems in its first year, mostly caused by its rather hasty development. Perhaps the best known is the floor section, which was lapped the wrong way, letting in water. Oil leaked on to the clutch, causing it to slip, a problem the early competition drivers had to learn to cope with. The transverse engine was also not only a little-understood novelty, but produced a certain amount of torque reaction which, in the early years, caused loosening

A 1971 publicity shot of Issigonis with some of his creations. 621 AOK is the very first Mini while in the background, AJB 44B was the 1965 Monte Carlo Rally-winning Cooper in the hands of Timo Makinen.

A poorly touched-up photograph (look at the badge) from the BMC press office of the Mini-Cooper, launched in October 1961. What they failed to mention was that the racing driver looking at the car was Bruce McLaren, at that time a member of the Cooper Formula 1 team.

The irony of it! The Mini was introduced to sweep the three-wheelers and bubble cars off our roads, and here is a three-wheeler using the Mini subframe and mechanicals. Moreover, it is called a Mosquito, the original name for Issigonis' Minor.

Dr Alex Moulton, crouching down (left), discusses his rubber-sprung bicycle with Alec Issigonis in 1964. Great friends, the two planned an Alvis family car which never reached production, then collaborated on the Mini. Moulton's idea of interconnection of front and rear springing was later incorporated into the Hydrolastic and Hydragas suspensions.

John Cooper and Alec Issigonis had known each other for many years before their two companies collaborated to produce the Mini-Coopers. Here is Issigonis sampling the cockpit of a Cooper Formula 1 car in 1961.

Issigonis intensely disliked Tony Benn, Minister for Technology in the Wilson administration, and everything he stood for, but he was forced to meet him on a number of occasions during the period when the Labour Government was bailing out British Leyland. This photograph was taken in Glasgow in 1969.

15

Enzo Ferrari had several Minis, occasionally delivered by Issigonis himself, who got on well with him. This is a special with additional driving lights at Modena in 1964.

of mountings and loud thumps on pulling away. Also, the exhaust was taking more of the strain than intended and pipe cracks were fairly commonplace.

There is a story that the Ford Motor Company took a Mini apart not long after it was launched at just under £500, and on costing all the items, decided they could not afford to build such a car. It was at least 20 years before they felt confident enough to introduce their own small car.

The very first Mini of all was totally hand-built by the Car Assembly Building 1 foreman, Albert Green. He had been assigned the task of building three prototypes, and labour

was in such short supply that he had to do the job himself. All the parts for the three cars were laid along a 220-yard assembly line, and he merely started at one end and made his way to the other. To everyone's relief, all the parts fitted and it is reported that just seven hours later Albert Green drove the first-ever Mini off the production line.

The body is numbered 101, the engine is numbered 101 and the registration number is 621 AOK (appropriately), and this car is in the hands of the British Motor Industry Heritage Trust and is often to be seen displayed at their Museum at Syon Park, West London.

CHAPTER 2

Design and development

Issigonis and Moulton

When the Mini was launched in August 1959, it bristled with innovations – transverse-mounted engine with gearbox underslung, rubber suspension, separate subframes, small wheels and generous interior space. These didn't just materialize out of thin air, but were the culmination of many years of design, development and experience – mainly by two men, Sir Alec Issigonis and Alex Moulton.

They had known each other for many years and had previously worked on a development programme for Alvis, who had wanted to build a large car as a hedge in case a contract for building Westland helicopter engines was not forthcoming. Although they first met in the late 1940s, after Alex Moulton arranged the meeting through a mutual friend, David Fry, it was some years before they worked together.

Issigonis was born in Smyrna, Turkey, in 1906 and had a Greek father and a German mother. His father was an engineer and designer who also ran a marine engineering business, mainly making boilers. He had lived in London for some time before returning to Turkey to run the family business. While in England he had taken out British citizenship, so when the First World War broke out he was disinclined to work for the Germans, who promptly put him and his family under house arrest.

The war passed, and just when things appeared to be settling down, the Turks invaded Smyrna, now called Izmia, which had been handed to the Greeks after the war.

First the family was evacuated to Malta and then they came to London, where in 1923 young Alec, aged 15, enrolled at the Battersea Polytechnic and studied engineering. Five years later he was out in the wide world taking his first job with Edward Gillett, inventor of an 'easy change' gearbox, which was superseded when General Motors introduced synchromesh.

Next, in 1934, came a two-year spell at Humber, where Issigonis was able to develop his interest in suspension design by building an experimental Hillman Minx with independent front suspension, later to be incorporated into Humber models. While at Luton with Humber he started to design and build his Lightweight Special, which was to be used for hillclimbing. He had been racing Austin Sevens for some years and with his friend, George Dowson, he decided to build a revolutionary car with independent suspension.

The project was not rushed and it wasn't until 1938, by which time he had joined Morris Motors, that it was finally rolled out of the garage and on to the track, proving itself (and Issigonis) almost immediately – it even beat Austin's own hillclimb cars, using the same engine!

He used a stressed body construction instead of the more usual chassis, and the suspension made good use of rubber as a springing medium – in that, a forerunner of the Mini.

Although he joined Morris to work solely on suspension, he quickly shook off the shackles and with a small team began to develop the Morris Minor, or 'Mosquito' as it was then known.

It was after the War, in about 1948, that the first meeting took place between Issigonis and Alex Moulton, who was experimenting with new applications for rubber produced by

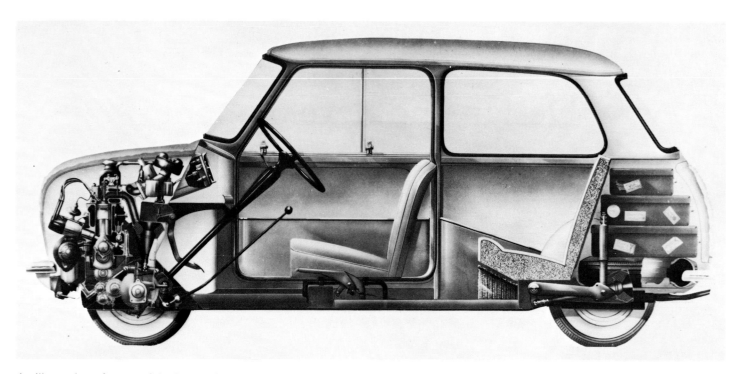

An illustration of some of the innovations that came with the Mini: the transverse engine and underslung gearbox, maximum possible interior space, novel suspension and small wheels. Other points of interest are the long gear-lever, storage bins in the doors and sliding windows. Note the little wicker basket under the rear seat.

his family firm.

Alex Moulton had set up a research department in his factory at Bradford-on-Avon two years earlier and, as an admirer of Issigonis, wanted to meet him.

'The initial meeting was not designed to drum up suspension business,' says Moulton. 'We were sensibly nervous of the high-volume car business. In fact we had been producing mounts and bushes for the motor industry for some time, probably since the company started in 1906. We had enjoyed "favoured nation" standing within Morris ever since 1926 when we had stood by Morris when he was in financial difficulty.

'When I met Issigonis he had already launched the Morris Minor, so it was to be simply a social occasion. We instantly hit it off like mad and, as we were both fond of Dry Martinis, we ended up quite drunk.

'Issigonis wasn't a bit interested in rubber suspension, passing it off in a supercilious way by quoting Royce, who said, "Rubber isn't an engineering material".

'I soon became a disciple, often visiting his flat and talking about design problems. I was struggling to develop and apply rubber suspension and we talked about my design ideas. I have never met anyone so enthusiastic and dedicated to engineering and design.

'We found in each other a great commonality of views, and although I have been criticized for allowing myself to become too much under his influence, I was bloody glad to have his guidance.'

Issigonis left Morris in 1952, fearful of the arrival on the scene of Leonard Lord and the formation of the British Motor Corporation, and joined Alvis to work on their proposed big car.

The Alvis prototype, although larger than most he designed, was a typical Issigonis car, being roomy and incorporating a number of innovations, including rubber springing designed by Alex Moulton.

'At the time,' comments Moulton, 'we were all agog with the notion of interconnection. Already there was a Packard and the Citroen 2CV using it, so we decided to develop it for the new Alvis, using a fluid for the interconnection.

'At about the same time I was involved in a project with Jack Daniels, at Morris, to convert a Morris Minor to use our patented Flexitor rubber suspension on the front and a thing called Rotashear on the rear. It was the first test of rubber as a serious suspension medium and it proved itself on a 1,000-mile test at MIRA.'

The parallel development at Alvis was also going well with a 7,000-mile test at MIRA in one week. The Alvis suspension used a Moulton design he called Diabolo, which looked like a pair of rubber cones joined together. Moulton quickly realized that these hollow cones could be used to displace a fluid, so he linked the front and rear of the car hydraulically. The BMC Hydrolastic and later Hydragas suspension has its origins in the Alvis' suspension. Incidentally, the Alvis project was cut when the aero engine contract did materialize, and now nothing at all, not even a photograph, remains.

This, then, was the background to the Mini project, which started with an invitation from Leonard Lord for Issigonis to return to BMC in 1955. He is reported to have said to Jack Morris, who was charged with the task of getting Issigonis back: 'He is the only man in the world able to design a completely new range of cars.'

Moulton remembers being at the 1955 Turin Motor Show in November when Issigonis asked him to join the team.

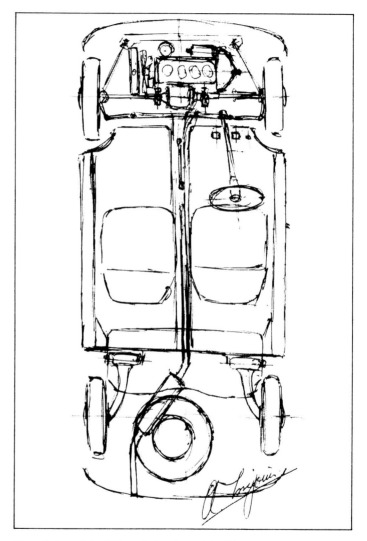

One of the original signed sketches of the Mini layout by Issigonis. Already it is all here: trailing rear suspension arms, transverse engine, small wheels and the radiator on the near-side. This sketch, though, pre-dates the idea of using front and rear subframes.

In the early days the Mini was built at Longbridge alongside the fading Austin A40. Here, a row of Austin Sevens are being checked off the line.

Spot the difference. Apart from fender rails, and a badge or two, there isn't any, although the cars are separated by at least six years; the one on the left is the original, that on the right being fresh off the line in 1965.

An early sketch showing the sub-frame layout and the location of the radiator. Initially the car was not designed with a subframe, but a 30,000-mile proving trial practically wrecked the car, so the subframe was introduced. Although a very neat concept, they do suffer from rust.

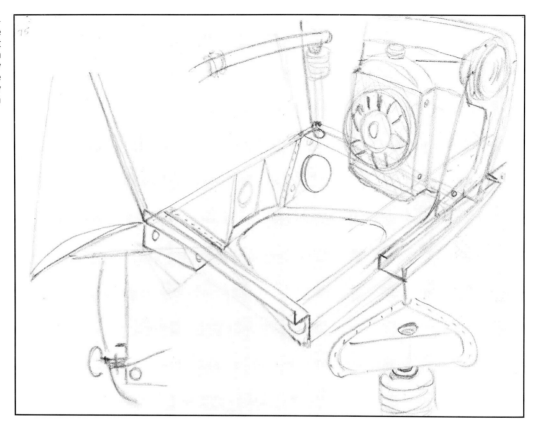

Moulton recalls the sentiment as being: 'My friend Moulton, we have some joint projects which could be of interest to BMC, including the interconnection'. Then Moulton adds more pragmatically, 'and he wanted my kit'.

By the time work started on the new range of cars, with the focus being on the middle car (codenamed the XC9001) later to be the 1100, Moulton had sold the Spencer-Moulton company to Avon, which was then partly owned by Dunlop.

Moulton then became a development consultant for Issigonis, getting his products produced by Dunlop for BMC, for whom he also worked – a neat circle, which meant he had control of all the stages.

Meanwhile, Suez broke and there was a swarm of bubblecars on the roads, which was unpalatable to Lord, who stopped all work on the medium-sized car and told Issigonis to go for the smallest one of the range.

'The Mini was absolutely Issigonis' concept', says

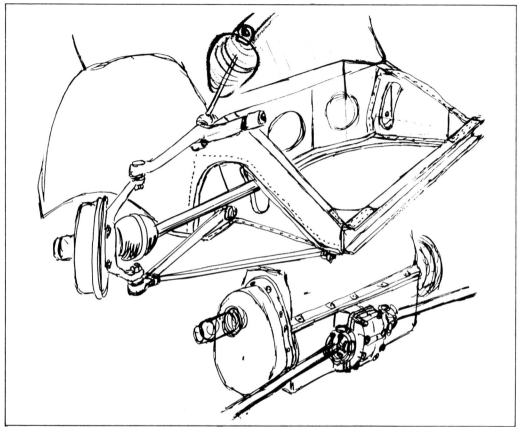

Having decided to use the transverse block and underslung gearbox, Issigonis had to work out how he could get both drive and steering to the front wheels. This is an early sketch exploring the drive-shaft problems.

Moulton, 'and his greatest invention; the gearbox slung under the engine, with both using the same oil, was prompted by an experiment he had made with a Morris Minor when he and Jack Daniels had built one with a transverse engine.'

Moulton is also of the opinion that for some reason, up to this point, Issigonis had discarded front-wheel drive, and if it hadn't been for Suez and the need to make the car as compact as possible, the range of cars on the drawing board would have been rear-wheel drive.

To build the Mini, Issigonis collected a small team around himself, and working by free-hand sketching, transmitting his ideas to the others, who would do their part of the job, allowing Issigonis the freedom of conception. He had an extraordinary way of being able to convey his thoughts by sketch and it is remarkable how accurate his drawings proved to be; in many cases the finished parts are easily recognizable from the rough drawings.

The Mini was designed with the arbitrary dimension of being no more than 10ft long, and because he wanted to seat four adults in some comfort, which meant a passenger compartment of 8ft 6in, Issigonis had left himself a mere 18 inches in which to house the engine and running gear. To achieve his criteria he had to do away with the gearbox intrusion into the car, as well as getting rid of the transmission tunnel. The small hump that is in the floor is to accommodate the exhaust system.

Initially, Issigonis experimented with a two-cylinder engine, effectively an A-Series engine cut down the middle, but it proved too rough and underpowered. Of course, with that configuration, the gearbox could be fitted on to the end of the engine, allowing it all to fit in the engine bay.

There seems to have been no great 'Eureka' moment when Issigonis decided to place the gearbox under a full-sized A-Series engine and thereby fit it all in, but it was a decision that changed the face of the small car forever. Of course, this idea had never before been tried, and there was

much fear from some quarters that debris from the gearbox would somehow get into the engine and ruin it.

As the story goes, Issigonis merely walked into the office one morning with a sketch and asked Jack Daniels to arrange the engineering.

Another brave step was reducing the size of the wheels to 10in rims, which had only ever before been seen on the bubble cars. They, of course, were much lighter and slower, so there was no problem with tyre performance. With the Mini there was no such guarantee. Dunlop went away to develop the appropriate tyre, not knowing for certain whether it would be able to do so, and make them to the short timescale available.

The Mini design went ahead on the assumption that the tyres would be available, giving vital extra room inside the car to achieve Issigonis' target of maximum interior space.

Meanwhile, the suspension was causing some anxiety, as

The cutaway of the Mk 1 Mini. Spot the floor-mounted starter button, the foot dipswitch, the long gear-lever and the subframes.

The availability of a suitable constant-velocity joint for the outer ends of the drive-shafts was a key factor in making a small but powerful front-wheel drive car effective. This Rzeppa joint design was developed from one used in submarine conning tower control gear.

Moulton was having problems with the interconnection. In fact, the problems were not solved for some time, although the basic Moulton design of rubber cones, developed at Alvis, was adopted with great success. It provided a neat solution to the problem of independent suspension all round without intruding into the passenger compartment.

There are considerable problems when it comes to suspension in small cars which are, by definition, light in weight. As a proportion to the weight of the vehicle a person is much heavier than if he sat in a large car weighing a ton or more. When four people are in the car the problems are even greater.

To achieve a suspension system for the Mini as sophisticated as the one they had used on the Alvis meant miniaturizing the cones, but there wasn't enough time. Moulton and Issigonis were convinced that the space-saving qualities of the rubber were essential to the success of the vehicle, but the problems of miniaturizing were proving too much. The eventual solution, to simply cut the cone in half and use it as a sort of buffer, seemed to be the answer, but would it work?

It did, of course, because of the innate qualities of rubber – it stiffens as the load increases. If it had not stiffened then when four people got into the car, the floor would have been scraping along the road. The interconnection idea of linking the front and rear cones by fluid was abandoned, but was to be used in the Mini from 1964. The Hydrolastic system was actually introduced to the motoring public in 1962 when it was fitted to the 1100.

Development was fast, and the small team had produced two Mini prototypes within seven months – partly due to Leonard Lord's enthusiastic backing of the project, which had been given priority numbers so that when anyone was presented with a drawing bearing that number they dropped everything else to complete the Mini work.

The first cars were hand-made and could have been spotted undergoing tests around the Cotswolds. Testing showed up some weaknesses such as that the forward-facing carburettor was prone to ice-up. This was solved by turning the engine through 180 degrees, but this would bring a transmission problem, which was solved by fitting a drop gear between the engine and gearbox to correct the direction

The principle of interconnection simply demonstrated. Alex Moulton, and later Issigonis, were great advocates of the system. It was not developed in time for the launch vehicles, which had to rely on rubber cones for their springing.

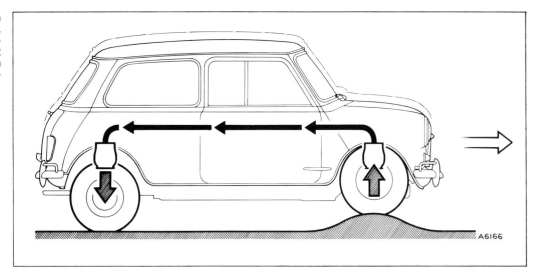

A6166

of rotation.

The additional gear reduces the power of the engine by some 3 or 4%, something that the team was happy about because the car was proving exceptionally quick and would easily top 90mph. This may not seem much nowadays, but in the late 1950s few mass-produced cars reached this speed, particularly small ones. However, the car was still too fast and the original capacity of 948cc was reduced to the now famous 848cc. At least it gave the tuners plenty of scope later on!

Other problems which surfaced during testing were the gear-lever amplifying engine noise into the passenger compartment, and the torque-steer. Both of these were solved, but one that didn't surface during the dry summer of 1958 was that a lip in the underbody was the wrong way round, and when it rained heavily, as it did in England in late 1959 and 1960, water seeped into the passenger compartment and soaked the carpeting and started to rot it. There were many proud Mini owners in the early years who were puzzled by the strange smell in their new car.

One further speed reduction modification made at a late stage was the insertion of 2in into the width of the car, although the reason was to increase internal space rather than anything else. This decision mirrored one that Issigonis had made on the Morris Minor, when 4in was inserted at a late stage to improve its appearance.

In July 1958, less than 18 months after the start of the Mini project, Leonard Lord test drove a prototype round the works. He was so impressed that he gave the OK on the spot, reportedly saying he wanted it in production within a year.

We do know he wasn't entirely sold on the look of the car, but after asking the opinion of Pininfarina, the famous stylist, he was told, 'Don't change it'. It would be difficult to call the Mini stylish, but it is functional, a view that pleased Issigonis, who regarded himself as an engineer and not a stylist.

His argument that if you styled a car it goes out of date has certainly been vindicated where the Mini is concerned. Thirty years on, it may not look so startling, but it has a following all of its own. The functionality of the design is most apparent inside the vehicle, although the flanges on the exterior give away the game to a certain extent. In the early models the spartan approach was taken to the extreme, with

The Morris Mini-Minor, while being identical to the Austin Seven in almost every respect, can be identified by its different shape badges and a different design of grille.

the single binnacle speedo incorporating the fuel gauge and warning lights, plus a few necessary switches set below, positioned centrally. Other oddities inside were the starter button on the floor, which had a tendency to collect dirt, and of course the 'walking stick' gear-lever. Elsewhere, there were the sliding (that is, side-to-side, not up-and-down) windows, the cable door release mechanism and the wonderfully practical bins in the bottom of the doors. The furnishings were somewhat sparse. A heater was an optional extra – only for the soft, no doubt.

At the launch, two Austin Se7en (sic) and Morris Mini-Minor versions were immediately available, the standard and de-luxe models. The latter included two-tone leathercloth upholstery and foam rubber cushions, screen washers, pile carpets instead of rubber ones, an adjuster for the passenger's seat as well as the driver's, extra trimmings, an additional ashtray and a lamp in the rear seat pockets.

Rather late in the development it was realized that a range of vehicles could be developed to accept the engine/gearbox, steering and suspension, so it was deemed a good idea to mount them on a subframe. The decision was also influenced by a 30,000-mile/75mph test run with a prototype, which suffered severe metal fatigue and nearly broke up. There was also a great deal of time spent on the development of a rear beam axle, which later found favour in motorsport, but the idea was abandoned because it would

26

A fine example of a Mk 1 Mini with its small light cluster, indented boot for hinged number-plate and light, and the bumper rails which disappeared with the Mk 2 shell.

take up too much of the room needed for passengers.

Other prototypes featured a gear-lever protruding out of the dashboard, similar to the 2CV and Renault 4, but it was thought this wouldn't go down well in Britain; besides, it gave a rather vague action. When the engine was turned round and the gear selection had to run from the back of the engine and through the floor, ironically this made the shift even more vague, but that was how the car went out.

Most people must also have wondered why the battery was located at the rear when it would have been far simpler to fit it in the engine compartment. The reason is simply that the braking was so efficient that the rear wheels tended to lock too easily under heavy braking, therefore it was decided to help alleviate the problem by putting the weighty battery in the boot, coupled with a rear brake pressure limiting valve from Lockheed. This ensured that a pedal pressure of 40psi was the most needed to stop the 1,288lb car in 75ft from 30mph.

Detail shots of the Mk 1 Morris Mini-Cooper showing light cluster design and bumper rails. This design was used until the introduction of the Mk 2 shell in 1967.

The famous sliding windows with their plastic catches. They ran in cloth covered runners, which often rotted away or became covered in a kind of moss. Note the interior handle, which eventually replaced the cord of original models. This was the trim material used on the Mk 1 Coopers. The chrome 'kick plate' on the bin pocket is to prevent scuffing the paintwork.

The Mini-Cooper was supplied with a boot shelf, rather than the rubber mat of the standard car, but both were supplied with a basic toolkit for changing wheels.

CHAPTER 3

Mini-Cooper

Production Cooper and Cooper S 1961–1971

John Cooper was a good friend of Issigonis. They had known each other for many years from the hillclimbing days when Cooper had been in his '500' and Issigonis in his Lightweight Special. Out of that racing had grown a mutual respect. Cooper had been the World Champion racing car constructor in 1959 and 1960 and for some time had been looking for a suitable car to give the Lotus Elite a run for its money. He saw that opportunity in the Mini.

In 1959, John Cooper was in Surbiton, running the company which had been started by his father Charles in 1935, and in 1961 it moved to larger premises in Byfleet, Surrey. Charles Cooper died in 1964 and John decided to take up an offer from Jonathan Sieff, the Marks and Spencer heir, of £250,000 and annual running expenses of £100,000 for the Cooper racing interests, although John Cooper remained as Technical Director. Disappointing results rang the death knell for the team and it was eventually wound up. Meanwhile, John Cooper had invested wisely and he re-opened John Cooper Garages at Ferring, near Worthing.

Knowing Issigonis as he did, Cooper was well aware of the Mini's development, and during 1959, before it had been launched, he had borrowed a prototype, taking it to the Italian Grand Prix with his contracted racing driver, Roy Salvadori. Not only did they beat Reg Parnell in an Aston Martin in getting there, but they had their views on the Mini backed up by the Ferrari chief designer Aurelio Lampredi, who declared, after taking it out for a long drive: 'If it were not for the fact that it is so ugly, I would shoot myself'.

With a production Mini in his hands, Cooper abandoned his original project of developing a Renault Dauphine, which so far had defeated him, proving itself to be entirely unsuitable for motor sport.

But Issigonis was against the development of his car for racing. The Mini was a people's car and although he recognized it was inherently stable and therefore ideal for competition, he was strongly against anyone tuning it. Cooper, equally determined, went over his head to BMC boss George Harriman and a prototype Mini-Cooper was the result. Cooper already had considerable experience of tuning the A-Series engine as it was also used in Formula Junior (today's equivalent is Formula 3) – a racing formula in which Cooper was particularly experienced.

The Mini-Cooper
The initial agreement was to build 1,000 Mini-Coopers with 1,000cc engines for homologation purposes. The 1,000cc capacity was easily achieved by increasing the 850's stroke from 68.3 to 81.3mm and reducing the bore fractionally from 62.9 to 62.4mm, thus giving a volume of 997cc. Along with a raised compression ratio, twin carburettors and better camshaft timing, the result was the desired 55bhp, giving a top speed of 85mph.

It is interesting to note that *The Motor*, in its road test report of September 20, 1961, entitled its piece 'A Wolf Cub in Sheep's Clothing' and then went on to say that 'the ability to exceed 85mph on the level would be highly satisfactory for a conventional saloon car of 2-litre engine size'.

30

The Mini-Cooper was introduced with a 997cc engine and with 55bhp it offered a tremendous improvement in performance over the standard car. The two-tone Cooper was otherwise almost indistinguishable from the 850 model, with just discreet badging and different grilles giving the game away.

John Cooper ran a very successful racing team, winning the World Championship two years running in 1959 and 1960, with Jack Brabham driving. They are seen here after winning the 1961 New Zealand Grand Prix. One of the other Cooper drivers was Bruce McLaren, and both he and Brabham, regarded by Cooper as amongst the best mechanics he had, went on to form their own World Championship-winning teams.

The contrasting styles of two John Cooper designs: a Formula Junior single-seater sharing his modest showroom with a Morris Mini-Cooper.

The long-stroke engine was seen as a positive advantage by *The Motor*, who commented: 'A very real advantage of this twin-carburettor long-stroke engine was its willingness to pull smoothly and hard almost immediately after a start from cold'.

With the engine size raised by 17%, the valves also needed enlarging, but it was found that they only needed a 12% increase, although double valve springs were considered necessary to increase the rev range to 6,000rpm. Other changes included a larger-bore exhaust and a slightly stiffened bottom end, and while changing the position of the gear-lever, Cooper changed the 2nd and 3rd gear ratios to make better use of the improved power and torque. The 4th gear ratio was retained because of the engine's higher revs.

The Autocar also regarded the car as having an impressive top speed, their testers saying, 'once the novelty of the higher maximum speed has worn off, most owners will find the main attraction of the car is its brisk performance in the important 40 to 70mph range'.

Having made it go better, Cooper also decided to make it

Eddie Maher, left, Chief Experimental Engineer at Morris Engines, where the development for the Cooper engines was carried out, with Charles Griffin. Maher had been instrumental in developing engines for the Cooper Formula Junior cars. The Mini-Cooper S engines were very similar.

stop more efficiently, and this he achieved by persuading Lockheed to make special 7in discs to fit within the front wheel pressings, replacing the original Mini's much-criticized drums. The effective braking area was increased to 104sq in from the original 55sq in. The rear brake pressure limiter valve was retained, albeit slightly modified to take account of the greater front-end braking. Initially, the standard drums were used at the rear, but in March 1963 the rear brakes were improved and in July 1964 a lower rear pressure limiter valve was fitted.

Although these brakes were a great deal better than the drums on the standard car, they were entirely inadequate by today's standards. But at the time, the magazines were full of praise, *The Motor* commenting: 'Application of disc brakes to the front wheels has certainly achieved the desired result of eliminating fade in severe conditions', while *The Autocar* said: 'Quite one of the best features of the car is the Lockheed disc and drum brake system. Moderately high pressures are required for small reductions in speed, but thereafter the action is progressive, with a reassuring feel'.

Externally, the body was hardly changed, although there was the immediately recognizable slatted grille, with 10 slats for the Austin and seven wider ones on the Morris. The other give-away was the two-tone paintwork, with the roof in a different colour. However, the Mini Super was soon given the same paintwork scheme, presumably to make Super owners feel that they, too, drove a hotted-up version.

Internally, there were changes which included a new vinyl-coated material plus a new instrument binnacle incorporating an oil pressure gauge on the right and a water temperature gauge on the left – luxury indeed! However, no rev-counter was fitted, or even offered as an extra, but the factory thoughtfully marked change-up points on the speedo to help the driver get the maximum from his new car. The markings were at 28mph, 47mph and 72mph, compared with the recommended change-up points of 23mph, 38mph and 58mph on the standard 850 Mini.

The extra engine revs and road noise of the Cooper were counteracted with increased sound-deadening material in the interior and round the wheelarches. The inherent engine noise was reduced with a 16-blade cooling fan.

There was still a lot of excitement about the Mini at this time, particularly from the press, which was still somewhat in awe of the little car's handling and roadholding. In John Bolster's *Autosport* report he enthused: 'The average speeds which can be achieved, particularly over difficult terrain, can only be described as incredible. The engine is very willing and the gear ratios are so right that even very fast sports cars cannot shake off this Mini'.

He then went on to extol the car's handling qualities even further, and gave a brief lesson on how to drive a small front-wheel-drive car quickly. 'What is so remarkable', he said, 'is the phenomenal "dicing margin" that is available. Most cars with high cornering power tend to be unforgiving. In the hands of an expert, they are most impressive, but the novice who tries to drive on the limit will eventually spin off ignominiously. The Mini-Cooper can be driven up to and past the limit of adhesion by quite a moderate driver. When he appears to be about to enter the decor he simply eases his foot momentarily. The tail comes round, the sliding car loses speed, and another burst of throttle sends him on his way'.

In January 1964, the 997cc Cooper was replaced by the 998cc version. The change in capacity was subtle and was achieved by increasing the bore from 62.43 to 64.588mm and reducing the stroke from 81.28 to 76.2mm, a more balanced proportion, giving a smoother engine. Although the maximum power was unchanged at 55bhp, it came in at 5,800rpm on the 998 version instead of 6,000rpm on the 997 unit.

The real gain was in torque, which went up from 44lb/ft at 3,600rpm on the 997 to 57lb/ft at 3,000rpm, giving an altogether more tractable car. The 998cc Cooper survived until November 1969.

Mini-Cooper S
Having seen the Cooper in action, Issigonis quickly became much more enthusiastic about the whole business of tuning the car, and soon he was actively involved in its further development. Having then realized the competition

Radial tyres became an option with the introduction of the 1,071cc Cooper S. Once again, distinguishing marks are discreet, with drilled wheels the main identifier.

JBL 494D, a successful 1,275cc Cooper S in 1966, winning the Czech Rally in the hands of Aaltonen, coming 6th in the 1000 Lakes, and 2nd on the RAC Rally with Kallstrom at the wheel, pictured here.

potential of the Mini, BMC knew that whatever they did had to be usable in the engine size classes which were (and still are) used in international events: up to 1,000cc and up to 1,300cc.

However, in 1963, Formula Junior single-seaters had an engine capacity limit of 1,100cc, and as much development work had been done on the A-Series engine to make it competitive at this size, it was decided that the next generation Cooper should be at 1,071cc.

To achieve this extra cubic capacity, the stroke of 68.2mm was unchanged, but the bore size was increased to near the limit of the block at 70.6mm. This over-square short-stroke engine was considered by some to be the best of the Coopers. It happily revved to 6,200rpm and could peak at 7,200rpm with its EN40 steel Nitrided crankshaft and toughened con-rods.

There were slight production problems. To accommodate the bores, a new block was cast with the outside cylinders moved out and the centre two moved 6mm closer together. Later on, this block was developed to exclude the tappet covers, which made it stiffer and allowed the development of the 1,300cc engine. Moving the cylinder bores not only permitted the use of larger pistons, but also the fitting of larger valves in the head. The A-Series block was not machined on a production line so the changes were accommodated without problems.

In the head, the valve sizes were increased to 1.40in inlet and 1.22in exhaust, 33% and 52% larger, respectively. In 1964, the pressed rockers were replaced by forged ones and the oilways were enlarged throughout the engine. The Cooper S cylinder heads can be distinguished by an extra securing nut and, if inspected, revised ports for better flow.

The gearbox for the 'S' was also modified, needle-roller bearings being used for the 2nd and 3rd mainshaft gears and improved bearings on the idler and 1st motion shaft.

When introduced, the 1071S used the Cooper 3.77:1 final drive, but an option was available, a 3.44:1 final drive, raising the intermediate ratios from 5.1 to 4.67, 7.21 to 6.59 and 12.05 to 11.02, respectively. The clutch was improved with bonded linings and double springs.

The 1071S Cooper used a fairly mild camshaft, the AEA630, but it provided a tractable 70bhp at 6,200rpm on its twin 1.25in SU carburettors, plus a good torque band between 3,000 and 5,000rpm, peaking at 62lb/ft at 4,500rpm. With its enlarged oil galleries, competition oil pump and 75psi pressure relief valve, the engine was ideal for rallying.

If *The Motor* had called the original Cooper 'a wolf cub in sheep's clothing', they admitted that the 1,071cc Cooper S was an entirely different animal altogether, and suggested that it rated as a 'full-grown wolf, in potentialities if not size'. Their tester went on to say that 'the car is completely tractable, giving as good a service shopping on Saturday morning as when racing on the Silverstone Club Circuit in the afternoon or rallying the same night. At a price of under £700 inclusive of Purchase Tax, this is one of the most inexpensive, most versatile and most exhilarating road cars ever offered'.

Once again, attention had been paid to the braking which, with the increased engine power of the 'S', was now inadequate. Lockheed increased the diameter of their discs from 7 to 7.5in and their thickness by 50% from 0.25in to 0.375in. This had the effect of not just increasing the friction area from 104 to 120sq in, but also improving the heatsink by a remarkable 80%, giving better protection against the old enemy, brake fade. Harder linings and pads were now included, as was a Hydrovac servo. As mentioned previously, the pressure limiter valve for the back brakes of all Coopers was revised to take effect of their lighter loading.

The 1071S was also the first production Mini to be fitted with wider wheels; in this instance 4.5in ventilated steel wheels were offered as an option, and you could have the 145x10in radial Dunlop SP tyres. Normal tyres were C41 crossplies of the same size, but they were no match for the

Graham Hill, right, was given rally lessons at Bagshot test circuit in Surrey by Paddy Hopkirk to prepare him for the 1966 RAC Rally in a 1,275cc Cooper, GRX 309D. Partnered by journalist Maxwell Boyd, he fared little better on the rally than in testing, retiring in the Lake District with transmission problems.

The Mk 1 Cooper had much more elaborate interior trim than later models, although the steering wheel seen here is non-standard. For the first time, the gear-lever was moved and shortened into a remote-control change. The speedo had a maximum reading of 100mph.

radials, whose only drawback was a slightly harsher ride. Manoeuvrability was also helped with the fitting of a higher-ratio steering rack, giving just 2.3 turns lock to lock, and long-distance driving made easier with the optional extra of an additional fuel tank on the other side of the body.

It was commented on by *Autocar* that overall fuel consumption was around 29.4mpg, which gave a range of only 150 miles on the standard fuel tank, and they suggested that the optional additional fuel tank should be fitted.

The much improved braking power came in for considerable praise, although *The Motor*'s heavy-footed tester said that 'the velvet touch proved particularly necessary in the wet when over-hard application brought considerable initial pull until the discs dried off. An emergency stop from about 70mph on dry roads, however, pulled the car up virtually all-square, with the slightest hint

With two almost identical models being produced, you had to look carefully for the identifying badges.

of wheel lock on the near-side'.

Then they made the telling and accurate comment: 'In all the Mini-Cooper S is a car of delightful Jekyll and Hyde character, with astonishing performance concealed within its unpretentious Mini skin'.

Externally, the car looked little different from other Coopers except for the discreet 'S' badges on the bonnet and boot, and it was this Q-car image that appealed to so many people. The 1071S was made between March 1960 and August 1964; some 4,000 were produced.

In March 1964, two more Coopers were introduced, the 1,275cc and 970cc versions, although their prototypes had been seen in competition for some while.

The 970S was probably the smoothest of all the Coopers and was introduced with competition in mind. A small overbore of just 1mm would bring it just below 1,000cc and produce an exceptionally powerful car which was nearly as good as the 1275S version. This latitude was perfect for the fast-growing engine tuners of the day, notably Daniel Richmond of Downton, who employed such well-knowns as

The Mk 2 Mini-Cooper S had a very plain interior and steering wheel. Note the speedo, which reads up to 130mph, despite the claimed maximum speed of Coopers never being above 98mph.

Richard Longman, Jan Odor (of Janspeed) and Gordon Spice.

The bore for all Cooper S models remained the same, the different capacities being achieved by playing tunes with the stroke. The 970S had a stroke of 61.91mm and a compression ratio of 10:1, while the 1275S had a stroke of 81.33mm (similar to the 997cc Cooper, 81.28mm) and a compression ratio of 9.75:1.

The 1275S had a tall block to accommodate its longer stroke. All engines used a crankshaft made from EN40B high-grade steel, Nitride-hardened by Rolls-Royce, and fitted with 2in big-end bearings, which allowed the short-stroke engines to rev to nearly 8,000rpm and the long-stroke versions to get to 7,200rpm.

The 970S was available only on special order, and from the outset the intention was to build as few as possible to qualify them (through homologation) for the International Group 2 Touring Car Championship, along with the other Cooper S cars. The 970S produced just 65bhp at 6,500rpm, but it was almost as quick as its big brother, the 76bhp 1275S, which was not as smooth nor as high-revving. The 1275S, though, had a more flexible engine producing 79lb/ft torque at 3,000rpm against the meagre(!) 55lb/ft at 3,500rpm of the 970S, so obviously it was preferred for rallying and racing. The 970S was discontinued in January 1965, as soon as a sufficient number had been produced to allow it to compete until 1970.

Motor magazine's heading at the introduction of the 1275S said, '...enormous fun to drive and just about the most practical toy that £750 will buy...'.

In their issue dated September 5, 1964, they said that 'Minis set their own performance standards and it is by these that we tend to judge each new specimen of the breed'. The Mini novelty was by now wearing a bit thin, so most of the testers were able to be a little more objective and *Motor* went on to comment: 'It has most of the failings of the other Minis – uncomfortable seats, and awkward driving position, bumpy ride'. However, there were still plenty of column-inches available for praise, and they added that, judged by other production cars of comparable price, it was a truly remarkable vehicle.

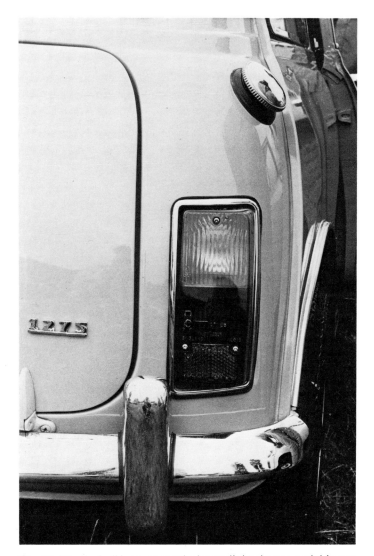

The Mk 2 bodyshell incorporated a larger light cluster, and this can be identified as a Cooper S by the '1275' badge and extra petrol filler cap, denoting the additional tank on the offside of the car.

Genuine
Mk.2.
Cooper
Grille
£35

Mk.1 Morris
Cooper
Grille
£57.50

At Mini Club days it is possible to pick out the genuine Cooper parts if you keep your eyes open.

On the Mk 2 shell, the grille was redesigned with the top chrome strip being attached to the bonnet and the sides reshaped to give the car a more pleasing look from the front.

The Mini-Cooper S was dropped, depriving John Cooper of the princely sum of £2 per car, and replaced with the uninspiring 1275GT, which, despite being less powerful, commanded the same insurance rating as the Cooper.

The villain of the piece? Lord Stokes was the man who closed the Abingdon competitions centre and cut the Cooper – not a record to be proud of, as it deprived BMC of competition success and international recognition. The company still suffers from the legacy of these decisions.

The best performance figures were reported by John Bolster in *Autosport* when he claimed to have hit the magic 100mph with his road test vehicle and recorded a 0-60mph time of 9 seconds, much better than the factory-quoted 10.9 seconds. These stunning figures may explain why in later road tests the same engine was guzzling oil almost as fast as petrol!

The Cooper S continued to receive the improvements fitted to the standard cars where appropriate, and these included the diaphragm clutch and, to the displeasure of most purists, the Hydrolastic suspension in September 1964. While working extremely well on the bread-and-butter vehicles of the range, the Cooper S didn't like the interconnected system very much, and there were constant complaints about body pitch. Most serious Cooper S competitors solved the problem by refitting the dry rubber suspension or blanking off the Hydrolastic units.

From November 1965, there were reclining front seats, and the twin fuel tanks and an oil cooler became standard fitments on the 1275S from January 1966.

In 1967, the Cooper S, along with all other cars in the

At the front of the car, Bill Appleby, the designer of the A-series engine, is obviously pleased with the outcome of the collaboration between John Cooper and Alec Issigonis, to his left.

Paddy Hopkirk's victory in the 1964 Monte Carlo Rally in a Mini-Cooper excited more public interest than any rallying event to that date. Looking on at the Racing Car Show in London are the three men who made this victory possible: John Cooper, Charles Griffin, Director of Advanced Engineering, and Alec Issigonis.

range, received the heavier Mk2 bodyshell and, in October 1968, the all-synchromesh gearbox. In March 1970, the Mk2 shelled Cooper S was superseded by the Mk3 Cooper S, which in turn was discontinued in July 1971.

The total production run of the Cooper S range was 45,629, with only 9,467 of these being sold on the home market, hence their rarity. Of the rest of the production, 583 were actually constructed abroad (in Italy), so a massive 35,392 were exported – 78.9% of production.

The ordinary Coopers had a rather different production record, with a total of 99,281 made between 1961 and 1969, 33% of which were sold on the home market.

By the time Lord Stokes drew the Cooper chapter to a close in 1971, 2,318,475 Minis had left the works. The best year for Coopers was 1966, when 18,000 were built of all types and 70% went for export.

John Cooper's agreement with BMC lapsed in August 1971 and Lord Stokes opted not to extend it, giving the spurious reason that the Cooper name was depressing sales because it was associating high insurance ratings with the Mini. The story might have been believed if the Cooper S successor hadn't been named the GT and hadn't attracted the same insurance rating.

At the time of the Stokes takeover, BMC was in serious financial trouble. It was having to fork out £2 for every car bearing the Cooper name – that doesn't sound much today, but the Mini was only ever marginally profitable and the company needed every £2 it could lay its hands on. Of course, in retrospect, the decision can be seen as truly short-sighted, but Cooper wasn't the only one to suffer in this way; the agreement with Donald Healey for the Austin-Healey was also terminated.

At the time the Cooper connection was severed, there were plans for a Cooper 1300 (renamed the 1300GT) and a Cooper 1800 (renamed the 1800S). There was one anomaly, and that was at Innocenti, where Geoffrey Robinson, then Managing Director, wouldn't relinquish the Cooper name as it carried considerable marketing cachet in Italy. Then he was transferred to Jaguar, in Coventry, and Innocenti dropped the Cooper name as well.

Cooper and Cooper S identification

Here are some useful pointers provided by the Mini Cooper Register which may help to determine the originality of Mini-Cooper and Mini-Cooper S models.

Mk1 Cooper

Chassis No prefix: – Austin C-A2S7
– Morris K-A2S4

Body

Duotone paintwork, chrome trim around door windows, overriders with corner bars. Original bootlids have fibre-board inside, secured by chrome screws and cup washers. All cars should have a boot board with four support brackets pop-riveted to the body. Safety boss fitted to door handles from January 1966. Austin grille has 10 slats, Morris grille has seven slats.

Interior

Check that opening for remote gearchange is a factory cut-out. Chrome gear lever and steering column support bracket. Three-dial instrument cluster – 100mph speedo with oil pressure and water temperature gauges with 'pointed' bezels. Black vinyl on top of dash rail and screen pillars. Chrome ashtray with solid lid. Seats should be duotone. Liners: grey or grey with gold brocade (silver brocade on early 997s).

Engine

Prefix 9F. If it is possible to look at the rocker gear, check for double valve springs. Head casting 12G 185 for 997 and 12G 295 for 998. If it is possible to remove a sparking plug, check that the piston has a flat top or 'D' top. All Coopers use twin 1.5in SU carbs. Early cars had separate pancake-type air filters and Metalastik crankshaft damper.

General

Dry suspension to September 1964. From 1964, Hydrolastic. 7in discs at front. 1⅝in exhaust; 997 has single box system, 998 twin box. Voltage regulator on offside inner wing.

Mk1 Cooper S

Chassis No prefix: – Austin from C-A2S7 384101
– Morris from K-A2S4 384601

Interior

As for Mk1 Cooper except for 120 mph speedo (very early 1071s had 100mph speedo).

Engine

Engine No prefix:

1071	9F-SA-H
	9FD-SA-H
970	9F-SA-X
	9FD-SA-X
1275	9F-SA-Y
	9FD-SA-Y

All S engines have removable tappet covers on back of block and 10-stud and one-bolt fixing for the cylinder head. Check for factory notch in rocker box to clear extra stud and bolt. 970 has flat-top pistons.

S engines have forged solid rockers and double valve springs. Head castings were originally AEG163, though many will have been replaced by 12G 940. Large one-piece crankshaft damper pulley and cutaway engine mounting bracket to accommodate it. Coil should have HA12 stamped on base. No vacuum advance on distributor.

General

As for Mk1 Cooper. Check for servo and that brackets look original. Most cars will have taller brake master cylinder (on some, however, they were the same size). 7.5in discs and built-in spacers on rear drums. Wheels are 3.5in or 4.5in ventilated by nine holes. Oil cooler standard from January 1966, ensure this is original by checking the mountings (two vertical brackets to the bottom of the front panels) and pipes (rubber-covered with brass threaded unions). Voltage regulator mounted on offside bulkhead on early cars – later on offside inner wing above the bulkhead.

Mk2 Cooper

Chassis No prefix: – Austin C-A2SB
– Morris K-A2S6

Body

Duotone paintwork, chrome trim around door windows, overriders. Body has 2in larger rear window. Double-skinned bootlid (late cars have Mk3 pressing). All cars have boot board, finished in grey (black on late cars), brackets spot-welded to body. Grille with seven slats.

Interior

Chrome gear-lever, three-dial instrument cluster with rounded bezels. 100mph speedo. Seats and liners black except for a few early cars. Black vinyl on top dash rail and screen pillars. Chrome ashtray with solid lid.

Engine

Engine No prefix: – 9FD
9FD-XE
99H 377
99H 378

Double valve springs. Head casting is 12G 295. D-topped pistons.

General

Hydrolastic suspension. Built-in spacer on rear drums. Late cars may be finished in Mk3 monotone colours. Voltage regulator mounted on offside inner wing.

Mk2 Cooper S

Chassis No prefix: – Austin C-A2SB
– Morris K-A2S6

Body

As for Mk2 Cooper except for addition of twin tanks.

Interior
As for Mk2 Cooper except for 130mph speedo.

Engine

Engine No prefix: – 9F-SA-Y for 3-synchro box
– 9F-XE-Y for 4-synchro box

General

7.5in discs and built-in spacers on rear drums. Hydrolastic suspension. Wheels are 3.5in or 4.5in, ventilated by nine holes. Oil cooler fitted as standard. Voltage regulator mounted on offside inner wing above bulkhead.

Mk3 Cooper S

Chassis No prefix: – XAD-1
Body No prefix: – B-20-D
Commision No prefix: – N-20-D

Body

As for Mini 1000 (look for larger rear side windows). Twin petrol tanks, overriders, boot board with support brackets spot-welded to body, boot badge. Body should have radiator cowling.

Interior

Black vinyl of dash rail and screen pillars. 130mph speedo. Trim colour-coded to body (very early cars have black trim). Seats as for Mini 1000.

Engine

Engine No prefix: – 12H 397F – dynamo model
– 12   398F – alternator model

Removable tappet covers on back of block. Head casting 12G 940 with 12G 1805 stamped adjacent to thermostat housing. Forged rockers, etc, as for other S engines. All-synchro gearbox.

General

Lockheed Type 6 servo. Other running gear as for Mk2 S. All cars should be Hydrolastic and have electric fuel pump. Very late cars should have 3.65:1 final drive. Voltage regulator (when fitted) mounted on offside bulkhead.

CHAPTER 4

Fame through rallying

The works rally Minis

The Mini didn't have a very auspicious start to its competitions career. Firstly, no-one at the Abingdon competitions department really wanted the car; it was too small, underpowered and didn't have the kudos of their Big Healeys. There were technical problems, notably the ever-present slipping clutch, solved by blowing a fire extinguisher into the mechanism, or if this didn't work, a handful of grit as well.

Although Pat Moss and Stuart Turner, both then little-known, won the Knowldale Car Club's Mini Miglia – 10 minutes ahead of the field – no-one yet saw the Mini's potential.

The works entered a three-car team, with the numbers TMO 559, 560 and 561, in the 1959 RAC Rally, but none of them finished. Then there was the Portuguese Rally, when they did finish but, along with other foreign teams, were disqualified for having the wrong colour competition numbers, whereupon local drivers were declared the winners!

For the 1960 Monte Carlo Rally, six cars were entered and only two cars retired, with Peter Riley and the Rev. Rupert Jones finishing in 23rd place. For the rest of the year things started to look good with even a couple of class wins in the Geneva and Alpine Rallies.

With just 848cc, the Minis were no match for the Renault Dauphines and Saabs of the day, but the team persisted and early on a decision was taken that drivers had to graduate through Minis before they got their hands on a Big Healey. Initially this didn't help the cause of the Mini, which was still not taken as a serious rally contender.

Even such notables as Erik Carlsson, who was starring round the globe in his Saab and later married Pat Moss, tended to disregard the little car. As if to back up all the prediction, 1961 proved a disaster, the only favourable results being on the Tulip Rally, albeit 1st and 3rd in class. It was a dejected team which returned to England after the May 1961 Acropolis Rally with one retirement and two crashes.

The competitions department operated out of the MG plant at Abingdon, where most of the competitions experience lay, particularly with record-breaking and racing. Appointed to lead the Mini competitions assault was Marcus Chambers, a large jovial man who was not only a linguist and lover of food and wine, but also extremely astute. It fell to him to examine the rules to consider how best to prepare the cars for maximum benefit.

However, at the end of 1961, the Mini competitions department was given a new leader – Stuart Turner – and almost simultaneously the 997 Mini-Cooper was announced. In his outstanding book *The Works Minis*, Peter Browning reveals that Turner felt that he arrived at the helm at the best possible time. The team that Chambers had built up was second to none; the Austin-Healey was a regular winner and the Mini competitions knowledge had reached a threshold which was about to launch it into international stardom.

Stuart Turner was already regarded as one of the best navigators around and had walked off with the *Autosport*

Paddy Hopkirk with Henry Liddon heading for 3rd place overall and 1st in class on the 1963 Tour de France. Here they can be seen on Mont Ventoux.

Navigator's Trophy three years running in 1957, 1958 and 1959, and in the following year had won the Monte Carlo Rally in a Saab with Erik Carlsson. He also knew what made a good story, having been rallies editor ('Verglas') with *Motoring News* and had written a book on rallying.

His enthusiasm for getting on with the job, combined with his serious authoritative manner, was contagious, and he quickly established himself as the boss. Success was not long

The first of three. Paddy Hopkirk stunned the rest of the world by winning the 1964 Monte Carlo Rally with his ace navigator, Henry Liddon. This car, which was only entered for two events, the Tour de France and the Monte Carlo Rally, is now preserved for display.

Stuart Turner, the architect of the great rallying days of the Mini, under whom the works cars had their most successful years. He left BMC after the 1967 Monte Carlo Rally, to be replaced by Peter Browning.

in coming.

In the 1962 Monte Carlo Rally, Pat Moss and Ann Wisdom won the *Coupe des Dames* and were 7th overall – not bad for a car which had only just come off the production line. A non-finisher that year was a young driver called Rauno Aaltonen, who made his debut with the BMC team by crashing his car on the Col de Turini. Unconscious in the burning wreck, he was pulled out by co-driver Geoff Mabbs to become one of the most successful Mini drivers ever, with wins on the RAC Rally, Tulip Rally and Monte Carlo Rally to his credit.

Following the good showing in the Monte, Pat Moss and Ann Wisdom won the Tulip Rally in May driving 737 ABL, which gave the Mini its first-ever international victory.

Rauno Aaltonen was in the vanguard of Finnish drivers and shone at any sport involving speed from speedboats at the age of 12 to motorcycle racing, speedway and rallying. He was also meticulous to the point of being fussy, and as Browning recounts in his book, he very nearly lost time on one rally because he wanted to check the tyre pressures with his own gauge in case the Dunlop fitters' gauge was faulty.

In 1962 Stuart Turner signed up another Finn, Timo Makinen, at that time so little known that he was called Tim O'MacKinnen by one Scottish newspaper!

1963 started off with a considerable amount of activity on the Monte Carlo Rally. They didn't win, but they gave notice that the Minis were on their way, with Aaltonen coming in 3rd. Paddy Hopkirk was 6th overall and two other cars entered both finished.

The Mini was nearly there, but it wasn't until the introduction of the 1071S, tuned with the help of Downton Engineering, that the Mini rallying legend was born.

With the Mini-Cooper, engine power had already been increased from around 40bhp in the standard 850 car to 55bhp, but the 1071S was a quantum leap – adding another 15bhp to give it 70bhp – just the right amount to put it in the winning position. The team was becoming more sophisticated all the time and as the power went up, so did the car's reliability, through the use of better parts and materials such as nitrided crankshafts, forged rockers, redesigned connecting rods, a double-spring clutch and many more developments.

To Rauno Aaltonen the new car was a godsend and he won with it on its very first outing, in June 1963, on the Alpine Rally – just one month after its announcement.

The Mini legend became established on the Tour de France when Paddy Hopkirk gave the large Jaguars and Fords a fright by coming 3rd overall and 1st on handicap. This was an extraordinary feat that catapulted the car and Hopkirk into the headlines. In France, BMC dealers were taking orders even before the end of the rally.

At the time the biggest event on the rally calendar was the Monte Carlo, not the RAC, and this was the prize that the team was gearing itself towards. By now the team had world class drivers in Hopkirk, Aaltonen and Makinen and they had been rallying the Mini long enough to be confident about its reliability.

1964 was the year that the Americans in their giant Ford Falcons had declared that they were going to conquer rallying and win the most coveted prize – the Monte Carlo Rally. They would have done if it hadn't been for Paddy

Paddy Hopkirk re-united with his Monte Carlo Rally-winning Mini, 25 years later.

Hopkirk, who started from Minsk in Russia and won a titanic David and Goliath battle. It was a relatively dry event, which didn't give the little front-wheel drive car any help. So close had it been that even Hopkirk could hardly believe he had won. Makinen was 4th overall and Aaltonen was 7th, rubbing salt into the wounds by helping BMC to the Manufacturers' Team Prize.

In honour of that win, the car, 33 EJB, was retired and can still be seen today in the Heritage Motor Museum at Syon Park, near London. Since returning from that rally it has never turned a wheel in anger. Although it is widely regarded as the most illustrious Mini, it only ever competed in two rallies, the 1963 Tour de France and the 1964 Monte Carlo Rally.

The next leap forward came with the 1275S which, although somewhat temperamental, was to give the Mini the winning way, notching up a formidable number of victories until BLMC pulled out of motorsport in 1970.

The power went up marginally to 76bhp but, of course, the torque was greatly increased over the 1071S model from 62lb/ft to 79lb/ft. By fitting a short-stroke crank and pistons, the capacity of the engine was reduced to 970cc, with the

Still in one piece, although the rally plate is a bit the worse for wear, Hopkirk's 1964 Monte Carlo Rally-winning car, showing typical supplementary lamp set-up.

A few extra instruments in the rally cars for the drivers to take in. Note the 120mph speedo and the extensions on the switches, which were needed because with seat belts on only a gorilla could reach the traditional-length ones. The red line on the tacho at 10,000rpm seems optimistic!

Timo Makinen (right), one of the 'Flying Finns', who pushed the Mini to international fame, discusses a works S with team mechanic Gerald Wiffen.

Large capacity competition tanks were used on the works rally cars with high-pressure pumps.

1-litre class of the European Saloon Car Championship in mind; in this form it produced 68bhp.

The 1275S got off to a dream start, and no sooner had it been homologated it was entered and duly won the 1964 Tulip Rally in April of that year in the hands of Timo Makinen – but once again it was by a short head from a Ford Falcon.

The only other highlight of 1964 was the survival of John Wadsworth and Mike Wood on the Spa-Sofia-Liège Rally – the first Mini ever to make it to the end of this gruelling event.

Champion Aaltonen

1965 would be an altogether different proposition, with a re-designed European Rally Championship with 12 qualifying rounds and around 20 teams competing.

Although this was to prove to be Aaltonen's year, it was Timo Makinen who made the news by putting up a stunning performance in the Monte Carlo Rally, giving him a win not only on handicap, but also on scratch. The

Servicing the Mini was a lot easier than on other cars – just tip it on its side to get to the hidden parts. This was a good trick for drive-shaft swops.

weather that year was atrocious and Timo, starting from Stockholm to acclimatize himself to the car in snowy conditions, got more than he bargained for on the approach to Chambéry. However, undaunted, he drove flat-out until he was satisfied with the car's performance on spiked tyres.

The weather simply got worse, landmarks disappeared and navigation became almost impossible. Paul Easter, Timo's navigator, somehow managed to see through it all, although most others were not so lucky. Eventually, only 35 of the 237 starters reached Monte Carlo within their permitted time, and Timo's car was the only one without any lateness penalties at all.

As usual, the remaining runners had to take part in the 400-mile dash round the mountains incorporating six timed stages. He set fastest time in five of the six stages, despite being chased by a Citroen DS and a Porsche. On the only stage he failed to win, the car had come to a grinding halt when the contact breaker spring in the distributor snapped.

They not only diagnosed the fault, but changed the spring, losing just 4 minutes. What they didn't realize at the time was that they had dropped the fibre insulating washer and, by some miracle, the spring had not touched the base plate which, if it had shorted, would have put the car out of action. It was only when they tried to restart the car to take it to the formal prizegiving that the problem was discovered.

By then, Timo and the BMC team were late for the presentation by Princess Grace. Was this an offence that the organizers could not forgive, so did they set out to ensure that the Mini did not win a third consecutive Monte? We shall never know...

The rest of the year was mostly up, but there were a few downs. In the Swedish Rally the cold got to the oil and the cars, whilst on the Circuit of Ireland, Hopkirk proved his mastery over the tarmac. In the Tulip Rally, a late re-

The pictures the BMC press office were never allowed to release for fear that it might show the Mini to be an unstable car. In fact, they are testing for the 1964 RAC Rally, although neither of these cars was entered for the event, in which all four works cars retired. CRX 91B came 26th in the 1965 Monte Carlo Rally in the hands of Paddy Hopkirk (he had won the event in 1964), and the car was later sold to Rauno Aaltonen. 18 CRX had competed in the 1964 Monte, when it retired, and in the 1963 Alpine, in which it came 5th overall. This car was later sold to Paul Easter.

classification made a nonsense of the event, then in the Acropolis and Scottish Rallies, Makinen and Hopkirk both retired.

Apart from the Alpine Rally in July 1965, won by Makinen in a Mini, Aaltonen put together the string of successes which were to give him the European Rally Championship. First there was the Geneva Rally, then the Czech Rally. Following Makinen's success in the Alpine, Aaltonen polished off the Polish Rally. There was a slight hiccup when Makinen beat Aaltonen into 2nd place on the 1000 Lakes, then came the Munich-Vienna-Budapest Rally, which Aaltonen won, but only when the leader Rene Trautmann had a piston fail in his Lancia, just 50km from the finish, after leading the Rally all the way.

The championship hung on the last round – the RAC Rally – and it was between Trautmann and Aaltonen. Apart

from the Trautmann v Aaltonen confrontation to settle, there was also immense interest in the battle between Makinen, who had elected to drive a Big Healey, and Aaltonen, who was in the Mini – DJB 93B (a car that was written off in 1966).

Makinen took a huge lead, but seemed to have put himself out of the running with a massive 'off' in Yorkshire. However, by the time the rally reached Wales he was back in the lead. 'Tortoise' Aaltonen now stepped up a gear, and with the pair of them leaving the rest of the rally behind they slugged it out stage by stage. The poor weather conditions favoured the Mini, and Aaltonen scraped home to win and take the 1965 European Championship – the first time a British car had won it, albeit in the hands of a Finn.

Then came 1966 and the Monte Carlo Rally

Perhaps the team should have seen trouble coming when the regulations for the 1966 Monte Carlo Rally were published in November 1965. There had already been one rule change by the FIA, the sport's ruling body, which stipulated that 5,000 identical cars had to be built in the preceding 12 months for Group 1, 1,000 for Group 2 and 100 for Group 3. As the Minis had always been run in Group 2 or Group 3 trim this didn't seem to matter.

One of the finest rallying teams ever collected under one stable. Left to right: Paul Easter, Simo Lampinen, Mike Wood, Stuart Turner, Rauno Aaltonen, Tony Fall, Paddy Hopkirk, Timo Makinen, Henry Liddon and Ron Crellin.

A well-campaigned car, this was the vehicle which, in Hopkirk's hands, was disqualified from winning the 1966 Monte Carlo Rally. It took part in 11 events, including the 1967 84-Hour Marathon, in which it finished 2nd. Here it is being driven by Timo Makinen on the 1966 RAC Rally.

However, the Monte Carlo regulations handicapped Groups 2 and 3 to such an extent that only a Group 1 car would have any chance of winning.

Peter Browning, later to be team manager, recalls in his book, 'Looking at it in retrospect it was quite obvious that the Monegasques were fed up with these little foreign cars winning "their" Rally outright twice in succession and were determined that they should not do it a third time. They were convinced that 5,000 Mini-Cooper Ss could not possibly have been built in the previous 12 months; and they believed that a virtually standard Mini-Cooper S could not win the Rally.

They were wrong on both counts, of course, but there had been a particularly hostile reaction to the British team's earlier successes and it was obvious from the start that scrutineering was going to be the most important aspect of the rally.

The homologation problem of building 5,000 cars in a 12-month period was solved by increasing the production rate so that, by the time of the Rally, 5,047 identical cars had been built, enabling the car to be homologated into Group 1. Although this first hurdle had been overcome, it was still unclear as to exactly what modifications were permitted by the FIA – they had issued three revised versions of the appropriate section (Appendix J) in the rule book. In December, Stuart Turner, then the BMC competitions director, made a trip to Paris, the home of the FIA, to clear up more than 100 points. He did not inquire about headlamp modifications as at the time the rules appeared to be quite clear.

The anti-British feeling was running deep and the French press was full of thinly-veiled references to cheating, with the finger pointing directly at the UK cars. There was a strong feeling, even by the pro-British camp, that the organizers would 'arrange' for the French to win, somehow or other.

Once the rally got underway, Timo Makinen soon hit the front, and found running at number 1 on the road somewhat frustrating, with roads still open to traffic and timekeepers at the control points still in the bar. With the Minis putting up outright quickest times, the hostility soon turned to disbelief and suspicion – and then there was slight concern over a headlight check, which had singled out the British cars as not complying with international highway regulations regarding their dipping systems. But nothing more was said or done about it and the cars were allowed to continue with the night stages.

By the end of the rally Timo Makinen had won outright, with Paddy Hopkirk 2nd and the Cortina of Roger Clark in 3rd place. As is usual, the winning cars were scrutineered carefully, but this time it was unusual in that the cars were literally taken apart, bolt-by-bolt, the engines stripped, and every item measured and weighed. All this took 8 hours, with the mechanics and team manager on hand to point out when the scrutineers were measuring incorrectly or referring to the wrong set of papers.

Eventually the scrutineers had to admit that there was nothing about the cars that was wrong. The organizers even had to issue an apology after claiming that the wheel track on Paddy Hopkirk's car was 3.5 millimeters (!) too wide. After being persuaded to remeasure the car the track was found to be correct.

Thinking they had satisfied all argument, the Mini contingent were convinced that they had won – but they hadn't allowed for the French determination, as, when the results were announced, the top BMC and Ford cars were nowhere to be seen and victory had been given to Citroen. When the organizers were eventually found they quoted the headlamp problems, but instead of it being against International Traffic Regulations they had decided it was now against Appendix J. Altogether, 32 protests were received, but all were rejected, as were the appeals all the way up to the Paris-based FIA. Surely this day must be the most scurrilous in French motorsport, and it remains one of great embarrassment to the French enthusiast.

There is an interesting postscript to this. One of the French motoring journals which had been leading the baying against the British cars was *L'Equipe*, so BMC

Sweet revenge. Rauno Aaltonen, left, and Henry Liddon after their victory in the 1967 Monte Carlo Rally. The year before, the disqualified cars and teams had appeared on the stage of the London Palladium and been feted as winners. In 1967, a special air ferry was chartered to bring the cars and crew home.

decided to pull a standard Cooper S out of a French showroom and invite them to test it on a timed section against a rally car.

L'Equipe nominated Alain Bertaut, a well-known journalist and experienced racing driver who, along with Timo Makinen, drove the two cars up a difficult hillclimb course. Much to their surprise, the standard car out of the showroom proved even quicker that the rally car, which was weighed down by roll bars and other rally equipment. This exercise did go some way to silencing the critics and proved that whoever was cheating, it wasn't the British.

Later that year

The rest of 1966 can best be described as having some good news and some bad news. In February, in the Italian Rally

of the Flowers, a Mini was again disqualified, but this was for an entirely different reason – Tony Fall having removed a paper air cleaner from the carburettor – but equally frustrating. Then Aaltonen and Makinen both retired from the Swedish Rally.

Things were looking grim when Hopkirk and Fall started off on the Circuit of Ireland. Hopkirk crashed, but Fall came in 1st overall. Then it was off to the Tulip Rally, which Aaltonen won, and to round off a hat-trick, Hopkirk won the Austrian Alpine Rally. Victories also came in the Scottish, the Czech, the Polish, the 1000 Lakes and the Munich-Vienna-Budapest rallies, and there was a 2nd overall in the RAC Rally for new driver Harry Kallstrom.

At the end of an eventful year, which saw the teams competing in 18 events, Stuart Turner decided to bow out

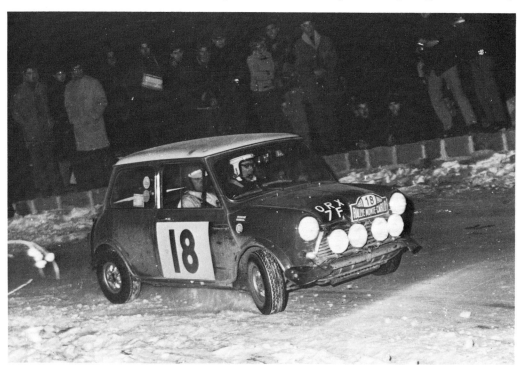

By 1968, the Mini was finding it increasingly difficult to win rallies, although they were often in the top five. Here are Rauno Aaltonen and Henry Liddon during the 1968 Monte Carlo Rally in which they came 3rd – the highest-placed Mini.

A classic Mini shot – a car built for the 1967 RAC Rally, but suddenly turned into a Rallycross competitor, being piloted by Timo Makinen, with Tony Fall holding on.

as competitions manager and went to Castrol, but not before the 1967 Monte Carlo Rally, which he was determined to win. His place was to be taken by Peter Browning, who worked closely with Turner to gain revenge in France.

This time there were to be no mistakes, the only drama being a rock appearing out of nowhere to wreck Timo Makinen's chances of victory. However, the rest of the cars were unscathed and Aaltonen drove to victory. Hopkirk was 6th, Fall 10th, Simo Lampinen 15th, and Makinen struggled in 41st. Revenge here was certainly sweet.

As far as rallying is concerned, that is almost it. There was

Paddy Hopkirk and Ron Crellin driving to 5th overall and 3rd in class on the 1968 Monte Carlo Rally having started from Lisbon.

victory for Hopkirk in the Circuit of Ireland in March 1967, for Tony Fall in the Geneva Rally in June, for Makinen in the 1000 Lakes in August, and for Hopkirk again in the Alpine Rally in September 1967. Although they weren't to know it, that was to be their last works rally victory – partly because of the usual breakdowns and accidents, but also because the rest of the rallying world was closing the technology gap and the Mini was no longer out on its own.

CHAPTER 5

Minis on track

Racing from international to club events

While the factory's competitions department concentrated on rallying, much of the 'works' racing was, in fact, undertaken by the Cooper Car Company, starting in 1962 when John Love won the British Saloon Car Championship. Cooper was the unofficial face of BMC on the tracks and was financed to a greater or lesser degree by the corporation, depending on the cash available at the time.

In 1963, Cooper ran Sir John Whitmore (who had also raced with them in 1962), Tim Mayer and, occasionally, Paddy Hopkirk. Although they failed to win the championship that year, they put up a tremendous battle, eventually losing out to a giant Ford Galaxie driven by Jack Sears. Meanwhile, a Downton Engineering-tuned car driven by Rob Slotemaker won the 1,300cc class of the European Saloon Car Championship.

The Mini was beginning to create a lot of interest for privateers on the track, and towards the end of the season Team Broadspeed entered the scene with John Handley and John Fitzpatrick driving. But they were not the only newcomers and in 1964 Ken Tyrrell entered a two-car team for the European Saloon Car Championships with drivers Warwick Banks and Julian Vernaeve, while John Fitzpatrick joined the Cooper team.

The results that year were excellent, with Warwick Banks winning the European Championship outright and John Fitzpatrick in 2nd place in the British Championship as well as winning the 1,300cc class. However, by this time Broadspeed had dropped out because of lack of financial support and was now campaigning Fords.

Of all the Mini drivers during this period, the best remembered is probably John Rhodes, who always seemed to have a slight edge over his fellow drivers. He started racing seriously in 1960 in Formula Junior, winning numerous races including the Formula Junior Championship of Ireland. Proving his versatility he also won the 1965 Guards 1000-mile race at Brands Hatch behind the wheel of an MGB, but it was in the Minis that he is best remembered for his flair and style.

With the merger of BMC and Leyland at the end of 1968 it quickly became obvious that one of the early targets for cost cutting was to be the competitions department, so the rallying team was disbanded and a racing team was formed instead. Paddy Hopkirk was on a 2-year contract and he remained to see out the few rallies that were left of that season's calendar. It had also become obvious that without the prospect of a new car the rallying programme was going to become increasingly difficult to sustain, and this fact certainly contributed to the decision to go racing.

So for 1969 the works team started off by signing John Rhodes and John Handley – two good men to have on your side in a Mini race. But their start was not auspicious.

The first race was to be at Brands Hatch in March and, despite having had to prepare their cars in a hurry, the team's initial testing run at Silverstone had been encouraging. The Brands Hatch race was to be run in two heats, but a startline pile-up in the first heat put paid to John Rhodes' car, wrecking it completely, while in the second heat John Handley comprehensively wrote off his, so

The master, John Rhodes, shows just how hard he used to work at winning his races. Here he is at Mallory Park on June 29, 1969. Many tried to emulate his technique, but no-one really succeeded.

At the 1960 British Grand Prix meeting at Silverstone a 'demonstration' race staged by the Grand Prix drivers. The cars of Jim Clark, Phil Hill, Innes Ireland, John Surtees, Jo Bonnier, Bruce McLaren and Graham Hill are prominent as the grid lines up for a few laps of hilarious on-the-limit racing.

Rob Mason scurries away at the start of a saloon car race at Brands Hatch.

In club racing this was what it was all about – a grid of mostly Minis blasting off at Brands Hatch.

back they went to Abingdon with a pile of bits.

It cannot be said that the year's results were particularly exciting because the cars, although generally reliable, were not as quick as the Escorts. Furthermore, private Coopers, particularly in the hands of Gordon Spice, proved exceedingly quick and often pipped the works team, for whom success finally came at Salzburg, in October, when Rhodes and Handley managed a 1–2 finish. As far as racing was concerned that was that, but there was one more area of competition that the works team was exploring – rallycross.

The Mini was finally eclipsed in the British Saloon Car Championship in 1980 when the regulations were changed to include a higher minimum weight which effectively ruled out the car.

Club racing takes off

For the club racer the Mini was a godsend – it was relatively cheap to prepare, it was easy to drive and it was exceptionally competitive. The BRSCC was the first organizing club to run a full class of Minis at the beginning of the 1961 season. While most cars were just 850cc versions, within a year the 1,000cc cars had become *de rigeur* and were thrilling the crowds with their close and exciting racing.

The Mini proved the great crowd-puller needed for club racing and on some days attendances of more than 25,000 were recorded. The reason was that the cars were generally so closely matched that the drivers would have to resort to a variety of sometimes dubious tactics to get a result. At one Mallory Park meeting the track discipline was so poor that the whole grid was lectured by the chief steward.

Out of this highly competitive melee emerged such names as Gerry Marshall, who went on to bigger things, and Bill McGovern, who later represented the leading edge of Mini development before transferring to Hillman Imps.

Minis began to dominate the smaller racing classes in the

Mini racing soon became known not only for close racing but also for spectacular accidents. Here, drivers make unconventional exits from their cars during races in Denmark and England, and in each case the crowd appears to be unmoved.

same way as Mustangs and Lotus-Cortinas dominated the larger classes, so rules began to be tinkered with to try and break the stranglehold of these cars. The BRSCC, which ran the British Saloon Car Championship, adopted Group 5 regulations, which effectively allowed almost everything to be changed except the engine, and even this could be extensively modified. Special cylinder heads, fuel injection, larger wheels, limited-slip diffs, five-speed gearboxes and new suspension were just some of the expensive modifications permitted under the new rules. The body had to remain unchanged below the line of the wheel hubs, but above it only the silhouette had to remain.

In club racing the Mini came under pressure from the Hillman Imp but was still able to produce drivers of note such as Mo Mendham and Irishman Alec Poole. To provide some variety to Mini racing, Poole drove an indecently quick Wolseley Hornet.

Others who were brought up on the Mini included John Aley and Bill Blydenstein, who were partners in the mid-1960s team, the Squadra Tartaruga, and prepared

John Cooper (left), Alec Issigonis and John Rhodes at Brands Hatch. Rhodes' most successful year was 1968 when, at 41 years old, he became European Touring Car Champion driving for Cooper. He was probably the most spectacular of all the Mini drivers and was signed up by the works, but with little success, winning just one race for them at Salzburg in 1969. He was partnered for much of his works career by another master, John Handley.

Steve Neal on his way to 3rd in class at the Guards International Motor Show 200 round of the British Saloon Car Championship in October 1969. Although he was not one of the stars, he was nevertheless one of the more successful Mini racers and was a works driver for the Britax-Cooper team.

Alec Poole, an Equipe Arden driver, was one of the very successful Mini exponents. In 1969 he went on to win the British Saloon Car Championship in a 1,000cc Mini, from the might of the Abingdon works teams as well as Cooper. Previously he had provided the crowds with a very hot Wolseley Hornet.

affordable cars for the European Touring Car Championship, thereby laying the ground for the later Mini Se7en racers. One of the names to emerge from that series was Tony Lanfranchi, who performed well in his blue-and-cream Cooper S. John Aley marketed Mini racers for around £400 to prove that you didn't need to spend a lot of money to have a good time and win races.

The 750 Motor Club devised the Mini Se7en formula, which offered two classes – full racers and cheaper restricted racers. In the latter class a small overbore of 0.040in was allowed on the 848cc block, with a standard five-port head, plus a choice of camshaft and a number of other modifications, all restricted by a carburettor which had to be no larger than a 1.5in SU. Limited-slip diffs were banned and the standard gearbox casing had to be retained, but brakes were unrestricted on safety grounds. The bodywork had to remain unaltered externally; although the front end

and boot could be replaced with lighter panels, steel doors were mandatory. Suspension could be lowered and slightly larger tyres fitted. This formula proved immensely successful and was the longest-running Mini class ever, although the up-to-1,000cc Mille Mini (later Mini Miglia) racing was also very popular. There was a good deal of experimentation in other classes with anything from 1,400cc Equipe Arden Cooper Ss to the aluminium pop-riveted ultra-lightweight car of Mo Mendham. There were short-stroke engines which would scream to 10,000rpm, as used by Peter Baldwin in 1969.

Harry Ratcliffe also experimented with some success, driving a de-seamed shell with a beam rear axle and an eight-port fuel-injected engine with intakes poking through the bonnet.

Alec Poole, a BMC apprentice, drove an amazing company-sponsored car, which was the state of the art in

Minis dominated saloon car racing for a number of years and it was not unusual for an Escort driver to feel rather overwhelmed by the swarm of them all around. Simon Ridge leads this Hepolite-Glacier Championship race in June 1970 at Brands Hatch.

Richard Longman, who had probably done more for Mini racing than any other individual, leads Martin Brundle's Toyota Celica in a 1978 Tricentrol Saloon Car Championship race.

1971 and showed what would have been possible had the competitions department not been closed down by Lord Stokes.

His Mini had a 1,293cc short-stroke engine with a compression ratio of just 8:1, an eight-port cylinder head, Lucas fuel injection and a Holset turbocharger, part of which projected through the bonnet. Under-bonnet temperatures were predictably high, but were contained with asbestos lagging and two radiators, one at each end of the engine.

Rated as 1,800cc, it was reputed to produce 200bhp and proved almost invincible, especially as the handling was also improved with a beam rear axle cleverly located by radius arms and an A-bracket.

Meanwhile, Peter Baldwin was experimenting first with four Amal carburettors on his 1,000cc Mini, then a Cosworth Ford MAE 1,000cc 'screamer' engine, which proved highly successful. In the search for yet more power he fitted a Ford BDA engine and transmission to his Mini in

Peter Baldwin in a 1978 Wendy Wools Special Saloon race. He was among the most successful Special Saloon racers, eventually abandoning the A-series engine for a Ford unit and a spaceframed bodyshell. Others who became extremely well known in Special Saloon circles included Peter Day, Jon Mowatt, Jonathan Buncombe, Steve Soper, Reg Ward, Alan Curnow, David Enderby and Ginger Marshall.

Malcolm Leggatt heading towards the photographer as he rolls down the track with his rear window disintegrating.

The Mini Se7en formula was born out of a need for a budget formula of racing for the hundreds of would-be John Rhodes. The Mini Se7en Club started with 850cc racing, but went on to create the Mini Mille or Mini Miglia (as it was later known) class for 1,000cc cars.

1975, adding a Clubman front, not for cosmetic reasons, but because it was needed to contain the induction system.

Others to emerge from the ranks during this period were Ginger Marshall, Terry Harmer and Richard Longman, not forgetting Niki Lauda and James Hunt, both of whom made their racing debuts in Minis.

In 1969, Longman was the champion club racer, taking 27 outright victories in his Mini, which was fitted with either a 1,300cc or a 1,000cc engine, depending on what the race demanded. Paul Harmer also adopted the policy of swapping engines to suit the race.

During the early 1970s, Special Saloons became popular at club events. Their rules allowed almost any mechanical changes while the outward appearance of the vehicle had to remain recognizable. With engine development becoming ever more expensive, attention was then turned to the bodies, which were built of a spaceframe structure and merely clothed in the style of the car that the driver wished to race. They became progressively more extreme and have included such bizarre vehicles as Ginger Marshall's Mini van. Today they appear in all sorts of shapes, but in reality few look similar to their supposed parent.

Rallycross

Despite its poor ground clearance, the Mini also proved itself in rallycross and private entrants such as Dave Preece were immensely quick and successful. He was beating the works cars with such regularity that they were forced to sign

Mo Mendham had one of the more interesting cars which had been deseamed for aerodynamic reasons and had been lightened wherever possible by the replacement of steel panels with aluminium substitutes, some of which were better formed than others. The car could never be accused of being pretty.

him up, although he claims they were never able to produce the kind of power that he could obtain from one of his own engines.

Rallycross as developed in 1967 was a made-for-television formula, providing rally stages in the round, with part tarmac and part off-road track. Initially it attracted rally drivers, but it soon produced its own specialists, including Keith Ripp, of Ripspeed fame, who will be remembered by many viewers for having one of the most spectacular accidents to be featured on television, involving several lurid rolls.

With Wills tobacco sponsorship in 1971, rallycross finally came of age and also crowned Preece's career by gaining him the championship. Despite reductions in TV time, rallycross has remained extremely popular, although the Mini has been superseded by the supercars of the 1980s.

As with circuit racing, when the Mini Se7en Club introduced a low-cost formula, the Thames Estuary Automobile Club, under the direction of Denny Baldwin

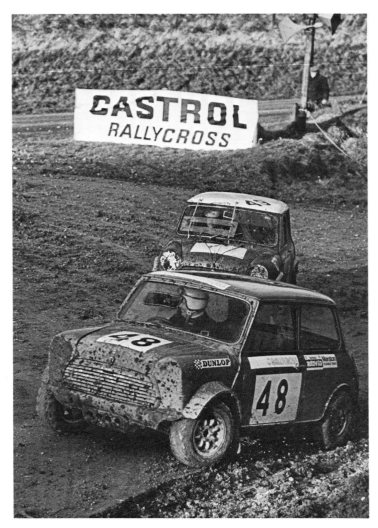

and with the help of *Cars and Car Conversions* magazine, formulated a low-cost rallycross series in 1978 called Minicross. This has since proved very popular as the technical regulations are heavily policed to prevent the formula from becoming too expensive. Another example of how the Mini can provide the basis for enjoyable but mini-cost motorsport.

Rallycross drivers went to great lengths to ensure that they could see out of the front of their vehicles because of the large amount of mud thrown up during a race. Here, Phil Cooper leads Graham Strugnell at the hairpin at Cadwell Park.

CHAPTER 6

Tuning up

More power for the sporting Minis

Daniel Richmond probably has the distinction of being the first person to tune a Mini. In fact his first successful Mini, with the appropriate number UHR 850, has been preserved and can be seen in the British Motor Industry Heritage Trust museum at Syon Park, West London.

Before the advent of the Mini, Richmond had built up his company, Downton Engineering, in the Wiltshire village of Downton, around larger and more exotic cars such as Lagondas, but immediately took to the Mini and, while the rest of the world was either laughing at the car or gaping at it, he was quietly working on it.

Richmond soon became a familiar sight at the factory, where he was to be one of the elite circle of men responsible for bringing so much competition success to the car. The others in the group were Issigonis, who initially wasn't keen on making the car go faster because he thought people were more likely to be killed in it at speed, Stuart Turner, then competitions director, John Cooper, Charles Griffin and George Harriman.

Richmond's contribution to the car's story, however, formed only part of his influence at BMC and later Leyland. Right up to his untimely death, aged 46, he was still being paid royalties for his work on the MG 1100 and the 1800S cars.

Downton Engineering quickly became famous for its engines and its stock-in-trade became the conversion of cars for the rich and famous. Richmond's clients ranged from Steve McQueen to the Aga Khan, and even Enzo Ferrari, a friend of Issigonis, had one of his cars.

According to Ron Unsworth, one of the Issigonis team who worked on the Morris Minor and later on the 1800, Richmond always claimed there was no magic in his conversions, just good commonsense and engineering principles. One feature of his workshops and engines was that they were always spotlessly clean, probably a legacy of his association with larger and more exotic machinery.

However, once the Mini was pulled out of competition by the works, Richmond's interest in them quickly waned and, apart from his consultancy work on the MG 1100 and the 1800S, he paid progressively less attention to his Wiltshire garage, devoting most of his time instead to his Devon smallholding, fishing and partying.

Ron Unsworth recalls frequently being invited to go fishing with him, and when Unsworth protested he couldn't fish at all, Richmond replied that his idea of fishing was to settle on the river bank and spend the afternoon drinking his way through a few bottles of champagne.

But while Richmond began to lose interest in the Mini there were others on hand to take up the challenge, many of whom he had trained.

Richard Longman, who once worked for Richmond and is perhaps the most successful Mini racing driver ever, set up his own tuning company. Jan Odor, a Hungarian refugee, who was taken in by Richmond, housed and given a job, eventually set up his own highly successful Mini tuning company, Janspeed. He was an excellent racing driver, and did much to give the Mini its reputation as a fun car to race. His company, still located in Salisbury, has now branched

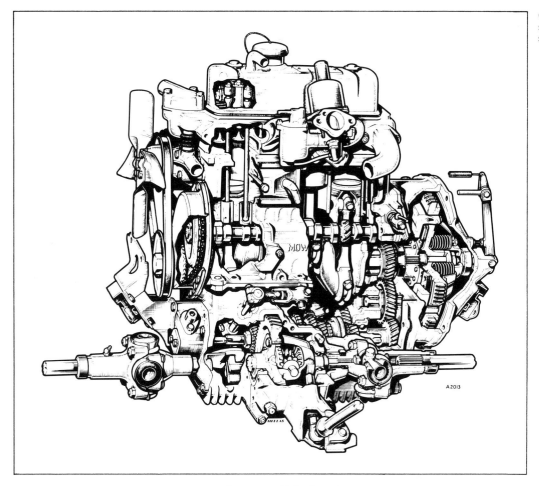

out into exhaust systems and is one of the handful of tuning companies which have survived the transition from the 1960s to the 1980s.

Janspeed has not only outlasted the vast majority of its former rivals, but was able to celebrate its silver jubilee with 70 staff and a turnover of more than £1.5 million, and continues to flourish today.

Disagreements over policy with Daniel and Bunty Richmond led Odor to resign from Downton Engineering in 1962 and, within a few anxious days, he rented an ill-equipped 225sq ft workshop in a local garage, costing just £5 a week.

By sheer luck, a former Downton customer, builder Tom Sawyer, came forward with the offer of £3,000 (and his

The key to the Mini success story, the underslung gearbox which shared its oil with the engine. The disadvantage was thought to be that the engine was more likely to pick up shavings and wear more quickly. The advantage turned out to be that the oil reached its proper working temperature more quickly and circulated better throughout the engine. This is a 3-synchro 'box with a straight-cut 1st gear in the centre of the picture. Don't tackle a gearbox unless you know what you are doing!

car!) to give the fledgling firm a proper start, allowing Jan to concentrate on what he knew best – tuning BMC A-Series engines for Minis and Sprites.

Within two years, Janspeed had moved to larger 1,000sq ft premises and it was on a notable Easter race day at Goodwood in 1964 that a Janspeed-powered car catapulted the company name to fame; John Fenning, driving a 998cc Janspeed-powered Mini-Cooper S, spent the day dicing with Sir John Whitmore in a Cooper Cars-entered Mini.

Jan Odor also campaigned his own Minis with great success. He was one of the earliest really successful Mini racers and he only stopped, by his own admission, when his own drivers, such as John Fenning, Geoff Mabbs and Richard Longman, began to beat him.

Tuning the A-Series engine

Everything in tuning an engine is a compromise. To begin with, the engine is made on a production line in large quantities as at as low a cost as possible. It is this last point that really explains everything. Take that engine and spend time and money on carefully extracting the maximum efficiency from it and you will see a great improvement. It is exactly this that the tuner strives for.

There is a great attraction in getting the most out of a piece of machinery. Engine tuning is a skilled job. But there is a lot the average owner can do just as long as he is prepared to listen to advice from those who know and accept that some work is best left to the professionals.

There is no point in modifying an engine that is not going

The Harry Weslake-designed cylinder head which has served so well. It provided plenty of scope for the tuners.

to hold together. Even at the very lowest stage of modification you must be sure that your engine is in good condition before you start.

The Mini A-Series engine is one of the simplest engines around, having a three-bearing crankshaft, a five-port cylinder head – three inlets and two exhausts – and the well-known heart-shaped combustion chambers.

Because of this simplicity there are a number of relatively inexpensive and easy modifications that can be made to improve the car's performance without making it impossible to drive on today's roads.

848cc engine

The basic Mini has undergone many changes, but the overall engine design remains the same. In common with other A-Series engines, post-1964 cylinder heads are better and by replacing the standard carburettor with twin semi-downdraught constant-vacuum SU HS2 carburettors, as fitted to the Mini-Cooper, it will instantly improve the performance. Alternatively, by fitting the 1.5in SU, as originally fitted to the automatic version of the Mini, in place of the 1.25in carb, the performance and output will be increased a little from 34bhp to around 37bhp (33 DIN). Be sure also to fit the carb's own inlet/exhaust manifold.

The 88G229 and 731 camshafts both work well in the small-capacity units, although on earlier engines it is necessary to have the block line-bored to accept three cam bearings. However, these engines are now rare, and you are unlikely to encounter one.

Cooper S-type Duplex timing gear is also a necessity once rpm start to climb. The Cooper-type tubular exhaust manifold is not suitable on this engine unless you are building a full-race 848cc engine. A long centre extractor, available from a company such as Janspeed, is a much better idea. A good road-going 850 Mini will give 60–65bhp without causing driving problems if you use the Cooper twin-carb head, cam and exhaust set-up.

997cc engine

This is probably the worst of the Cooper engines although the power can be raised to around 80bhp by using 1.5in SUs, a hotter camshaft such as the 88G229 (or C-AEA 731), an extractor manifold and modified cylinder head, but you will have to be careful as the bottom end of the engine is not too strong and will not take more than 6,500 revs with comfort.

The cylinder head design is not good, and if any of these engines are still in good running order (production ended in late 1963) they are best left alone or replaced. But whatever

The Mini-Cooper's fully equipped front subframe fitted to the 997cc car in 1961. Engine breathing has been improved with the wire mesh air intake filters and the long centre branch exhaust manifold. This was the first time the remote gearchange had been seen.

you do, don't scrap the engine, as the parts are still in high demand.

998cc engine

One of the best of the A-Series engines. It originally appeared in single-carburettor form on the Riley and Wolseley Minis, was then used in the 998cc Cooper and finally in the Mini 1000 and Clubman. It is a stronger unit than the 848cc engine, with a good cylinder head design on all but the pre-1964 engines.

Once again single-carb engines will benefit from Cooper carburation, but – like the earlier 997 – the three-branch Cooper exhaust manifold can easily be improved upon with one from a specialist. You can also use Cooper domed pistons to increase the compression ratio.

The first step to extra power on a single-carb unit is a modified cylinder head with either a single 1.5in SU, first-stage tune, or twin 1.25 SUs from the Cooper. The 88G229 camshaft works well in this engine as a road/rally grind, while the full-race C-AEA 648 is really a bit too lumpy and needs twin 1.5in or even twin 1.75in SUs to extract all the power.

The best fast road tune for a 998cc engine (also good for weekend competition) is a well-modified head, 88G229 (or C-AEA 731) cam, good extractor manifold, twin 1.5in SUs and a Cooper S distributor. At this stage, a Duplex timing chain and gears are essential, as is a crankshaft pulley damper (from an 1100), an oil cooler and competition centre plate to the clutch. Power can be in the region of 80–85bhp on a good engine, while in full-race trim around

90–95bhp is possible.

1,098cc engine

Pre-1964 engines (which includes early MG 1100s) can be put into the same category as the 997cc Cooper. Not particularly strong and well worth considering replacing – otherwise, follow the same tuning pattern.

From 1964, the 1100 engine used an important cylinder head – 12G295 casting – which is one of the most useful of all heads, giving excellent results when fitted to all earlier engines.

Again, single small-carb units will gain from the fitting of a single 1.5in SU or the Cooper 1.25in twin carbs.

If you wish to go further, follow the standard A-Series pattern of modifying head, fitting an extractor exhaust and a hotter cam.

1,275cc engine

The non-S 1,275cc engine is quite strong and provides a good basis for further tuning. All single-carb units use the 1.5in SU, so the first stage of the tune can be to go for a well-modified cylinder head and extractor exhaust manifold. Then you can consider the twin 1.25in SU set-up used on the 1275S or the 1300GT. You may also like to 'steal' the Marina 1300 set-up which, with a modified head and twin 1.25 SUs and exhaust manifold, makes an extremely tractable engine.

Like Mini 848s and 998s, the 1300 engine in later form

Twin 1.25in SU carburettors as fitted to the early Mini-Coopers. The wire mesh air filters were later replaced by a more conventional set-up. Note the heat shield protecting the float chambers.

A 45DCOE Weber carburettor, as used by the works team, can be extremely beneficial if more power is wanted without too many other modifications.

uses the star-shaped oil pump rather than a pin drive. This, of course, affects the camshaft design and so the good old Leyland cams take on different part numbers:

Pin drive		Star drive
88G229	=	C-AEG 567
C-AEA 731	=	C-AEG 800
C-AEA 648	=	C-AEG 529

The five-port head engine is capable of around 95–100bhp in race or rally tune with twin 1.5in SUs. Twin 1.75in SUs can also be used, but these tend to improve power at the top end of the range at the expense of lower engine speeds. A better solution is a single 45 DOCE Weber dual-choke side-draught carb, which is probably worth at least another 5bhp.

If you want still further improvement, you will have to consider the competition-only eight-port crossflow cylinder head, which is quite costly as it requires a new camshaft, pushrods, inlet and exhaust manifolds and new carburation over and above the head itself. Twin 45 DOCE Webers,

Dellortos or Amals can be used on this set-up. There was also quite a fashion for the Fish-type carburettor, which may still be worth considering.

Cooper S

The S engines are already designed as competition units and will therefore stand a lot more power than other A-Series engines. The early 1,071cc unit was a bit of a strange size, but the 970cc and the 1,275cc engines were produced specifically to get under the 1,000cc and 1,300cc class limits – in both cases a 0.020in extra bore takes the capacity right up to the maximum figure.

The cylinder heads are pretty good and, for anything but pure racing, only require cleaning up by a tuning specialist. Cams in all cases are fairly mild and can be replaced by the appropriate Special Tuning grind, while larger SUs (twin 1.5in) or a single 45 DOCE Weber work well along with a long centre branch extractor manifold. The ultimate, of course, is the eight-port set-up previously mentioned.

A good road-going tune for a 1275S (which is by far the nicest road or rally car) is twin 1.5in SUs, an extractor exhaust manifold and a road/rally cam such as the 88G229 or equivalent.

Quick reference guide

Capacity	Bore	Stroke	CR	Carburation	Power	Car
848cc	62.9mm	68.2mm	8.3:1	1x1.25in SU	34bhp	Mini 850
997cc	62.4mm	81.2mm	9.0:1	2x1.25in SU	55bhp	Cooper
998cc	64.5mm	76.2mm	8.3:1	1x1.25in SU	38bhp	Mini 1000
998cc	64.5mm	76.2mm	9.0:1	2x1.25in SU	55bhp	Cooper
1,098cc	64.5mm	83.7mm	8.5:1	1x1.25in SU	48bhp	Mini 1100
1,275cc	70.6mm	81.2mm	8.8:1	1x1.50in SU	58bhp	1275GT

S-Series engines

970cc	70.6mm	61.9mm	9.75:1	2x1.25in SU	65bhp	Cooper S
1,071cc	70.6mm	68.26mm	9.0:1	2x1.25in SU	67bhp	Cooper S
1,275cc	70.6mm	81.3mm	9.5:1	2x1.25in SU	75bhp	Cooper S

With all the faults of the BL range of cars, there was one major advantage – most of the engine parts were interchangeable, as were many other items.

The rules for tuning and conversion are fairly straightforward and involve mostly commonsense: swap complete units wherever possible, measure everything carefully, particularly heads, where valve sizes can cause major headaches. Also always check your waterway alignments when putting bigger-valve heads on smaller engines. Don't forget that the Marina and Allegro both used the A-Series engine.

Cylinder heads are likely to be the most important area of change, so follow this guide:

2A629: The basic 850 head, also available from the Morris Minor, Austin A35 and A40.

12A1456: Similar to the 2A629, but without water temperature boss and fitted to the later 850 and 1,000cc cars.

12G185: From the 997cc Cooper and can be fitted to the 850 and 1000 (998cc) engines if bigger valves are required.

12G202: Similar to the 12G185 and found mostly on the 1100 model range.

12G206: Rare and improved version of the 12G202 – usually found on the early MG 1100.

12G295: A stalwart of the tuners of the 1,000cc engines. This head is found on the 998cc Cooper, MG 1100, some Mk2 Midgets and Sprites.

12G940: The nine-stud head ideal for big-valve engines and probably the most sought-after casting. Two additional studs can be added for the high-power engines. It is found on the 1275GT, 1300 saloons, Mk3 Midget, Mk4 Sprite and the 1,300cc Marina.

12G940: 11-stud head from the Austin 1300GT, Mk2 MG 1300 and 1275 Cooper S. Same head as above but with the extra studs. This is *the* head for the serious tuner.

Gearboxes

For competition or for fast road use, the best gearbox is without doubt the Austin 1300GT unit, which is an ideal substitute for the Cooper boxes. The basic rule is to try and

Girling were persuaded to develop this tiny disc brake for the Mini-Cooper. Although widely regarded at the time as a great improvement, it was in fact quite inefficient and it wasn't until the introduction of the slightly larger disc on the Cooper S that these brakes became truly effective on the Mini.

swop complete boxes rather than try swopping gears from one type of box to another. There were changes in helix angles which could cause considerable problems.

In 1968, the all-synchromesh gearbox was introduced, which also meant a change of casing, so there is a distinct division pre- and post-1968.

The remote-control and rod-gearchange boxes don't adapt easily so are best left as they were built.

Brakes

If you are trying to uprate your brakes there could be more problems than you might imagine. For instance, Cooper S brakes on the 850cc vehicles without changing the master cylinder might result in a sudden loss of pedal when the pads become worn.

Cooper and 1275GTs had dedicated drive flanges, hubs and constant-velocity joints and require a master cylinder with a bigger reservoir. All Cooper, S and 1275GT cars had a longer travel on the pedal (and consequently longer pushrods) so make sure all the required parts are fitted.

The tiny front discs of the original (997cc) Mini-Coopers were barely adequate for the standard car when in good condition, so an engine modification should be accompanied by uprating. A Cooper S set-up can be substituted complete.

Discs from the 1100 and 1300 model range are also problematical because of the 12in wheels and different constant velocity joints.

Finally, watch for Cooper S wheels on a standard car as the offset is different and they will foul the wheelarches.

The amazing fuel-injected cross-flow-head Mini built for the 1967 RAC Rally, the event which was cancelled due to an outbreak of foot and mouth disease. However, the development, for Makinen's car, was not wasted as it became standard equipment on the works racing cars.

The standard works set-up in 1967 included a bit of extra wiring for the spotlights, 'idiot proof' spotting on the plug leads and the 45DCOE Weber carburettor.

CHAPTER 7

Classic status

Buying and restoring a Mini-Cooper

The Mini is one of the few cars which has become a classic while still in production, so the Mini enthusiast is in the happy position of being able to buy most parts with relative ease, depending on the age and model.

It is more difficult to get parts for the most sought-after models, such as the Coopers, so when buying a Mini this should be borne in mind. For instance, the interior trim is now impossible to find, although there are some fairly good efforts being made to try and match the material and colours. The shell is probably the most difficult item, so great care should be taken when buying an early car to determine exactly what you will have to do to keep the car on the road.

Minis were made long before the trend towards comprehensive rust-proofing, so the rust-box reputation of early cars is apt. The construction of the car encouraged rust – there are numerous corners and nooks and crannies which the tin worm enjoys inhabiting.

The Mini's unitary construction in which all sections are welded together means that most sections are needed for rigidity and safety. For instance, once the sills start rusting the torsional rigidity of the body begins to go and this in turn exacerbates the corrosion problems.

On inspection of the vehicle, you may find that there is so much welding and plating to do that it is pointless repairing the car, in which case the answer may be the purchase of a complete new shell. The problem here is finding the right one for the age of the car. Early shells are no longer available, so if absolute originality is wanted, repairing the old shell could well be the only answer.

Because of their box construction, Mini shells are difficult to repair, with access to some areas being extremely tricky. If you are keeping the old shell, the only answer is to cut out the old and rusty panels and weld in new ones. Careful cutting and plating, then lead-filling, will do the trick, but it is a time-consuming and a highly skilled job.

That is the reality and it is no use pretending otherwise. But if it sounds discouraging, remember that most other 1960s monocoques are more complicated and proportionally more difficult to repair. The relative simplicity of the Mini shell, with its turned-out flanges, makes it a better proposition for restoration than many.

Many of the replacement parts are available through Unipart, and those that are not may be supplied through a British Motor Heritage-approved specialist such as Mini Spares who, apart from supplying Unipart and BMH parts, are remanufacturing their own and have a comprehensive catalogue detailing availability. Most of these parts are reasonably priced.

A word of warning, though. The cheaper parts are not necessarily the best value, and as more people come into the Mini market and start manufacturing their own parts the quality is bound to be variable. Go only to reputable suppliers and then shop around for the right part.

The money saved on buying a second-grade part is soon swallowed up in the time taken to fit and juggle it into position. Where possible use original parts or Heritage Approved parts, which not only meet the quality standards

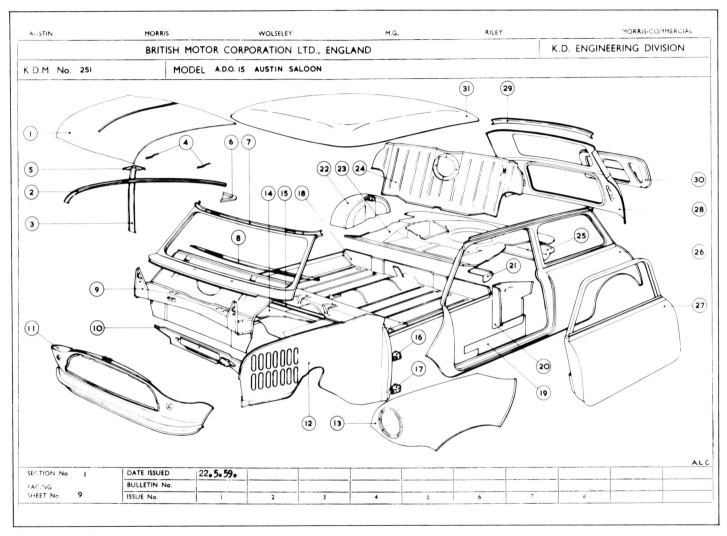

BRITISH MOTOR CORPORATION LTD., ENGLAND

K.D. ENGINEERING DIVISION

K.D.M No. 251

MODEL A.D.O. 15 AUSTIN SALOON

SECTION No 1

FACING
SHEET No 9

DATE ISSUED	22.5.59.							
BULLETIN No.								
ISSUE No.	1	2	3	4	5	6	7	8

A.L.C

An exploded diagram of the major pressings, which were simply welded together to make up the Mini, codenamed ADO15. This form of construction was ideal at the time because of the short lead time available from prototype to volume production. The method of construction has barely changed in 30 years and the Mini is probably the last mass-production car built in this way, with so much hand-welding required.

laid down by Austin Rover, but will also help to keep your car in as near-original condition as is possible.

A good example of the short cuts some people take is the pop-riveting of sills over old ones, or indeed the welding on of sills over the rusty parts. You can normally tell when this has been done by gaps under the door or the appearance of the sill when viewed from the wheelarches.

One of the problems from which the Mini has suffered is the dreaded filler. The Mini has done more for Isopon than almost any other vehicle. The areas most at risk are much as you would expect, namely the sills, flanges, front wings, front lights, rear valance and subframe mountings.

Sills
If the sill has been neglected for some time, the rust is likely to spread not just to the inner wing, but also to the doorstep and the floorpan, so when looking for a Mini, take care in inspecting these areas. A good Mini may have a rusty sill, but if it has been looked after the rust should not have spread. With relatively cheap parts still available from a

number of sources these jobs should not be particularly costly to have done, although labour will be the major element on the bill.

Doors
Having checked the sill and surrounding area, next look at the base of the door, which is particularly prone to rusting. On the older cars with the bin in the door they are quite likely to have some sort of rusting because of water collecting in the bins. Once again replacement skins are available, but it may be cheaper to replace the whole door rather than go to the expense of getting the skins changed. When checking the hinges you may have your mind made up for you; the old-style hinges which stand proud of the door are more likely to rust than the later flush ones.

Although the hinges may rust on the door, the most likely rust area is the A-panel to which they are attached. If this has gone, only a welded-in replacement will do – no amount of filler will fix this as it is load-bearing round the hinge and therefore will always come away after a short time. Once

'I need this like a hole in the head', was Richard Mansfield's first thought when he saw this dilapidated Mini-Cooper for the first time. No longer in its original Fiesta Yellow colour, the previous owner had used it to store animal feed and old engine parts. It had also been home to a nesting mouse. Two years of exposure to the rigours of the Welsh weather had taken their toll. Heavy rust could be seen everywhere. It cost £80 to buy and a further £2,800 and nearly two years to restore.

The engine was a non-standard 850cc unit, although it still retained the original Cooper head, carburettors and other ancillaries. The engine was stripped of all its Cooper parts and then discarded along with both doors, boot-lid and old carpets. The interior was totally original bar the brocade door panels, which had been discarded when the original doors had been replaced.

The panelwork required to bring the car back to spec was nothing short of drastic. Virtually the whole front end including inner and outer A-panels had to be replaced. The rusty panels were cut back to good metal so that the new panels could be welded in place.

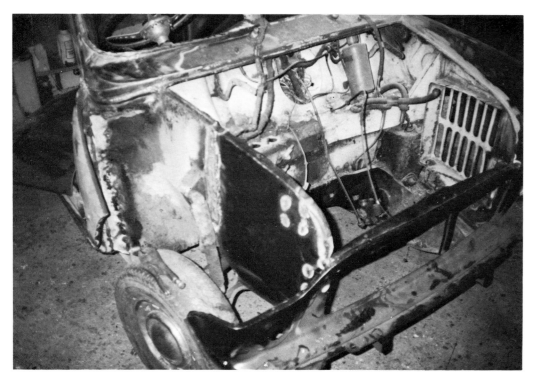

you start work on this area you may well find the problems are much more serious than you thought. For instance, the inner panel and splashguard are probably also rusty and the bottom of the A-pillar may well be suffering.

Guttering and seams
The guttering and seams round the car do suffer from rust, but generally not to the degree of the sheet panel items, so can usually be treated and will rarely need extensive work. The seams are relatively easy to replace, but the guttering is a much more difficult proposition.

Further up the door, on the earlier cars there is often rust on the sliding window mechanism, and quite often there is a messy mould if the car has stood around for a while or the windows have not been used very often.

Back of the car
Moving to the back of the car, the rear valance is often corroded, but this is replaceable, assuming the panel to which it is attached, under the boot, is in good condition. If there is rust all the way round the back it is quite likely that the rear floorpan is also rusty and the boot floor may be eaten through. The rear quarter-panel is a frequent casualty, as are the wheelarches.

The bootlid is once again a perfect spot for rust, particularly round the hinges. Take care to check the boot hinge mounting panel as this, too, is a prime candidate.

The front
The front wings are particularly prone to rusting, both round the area below the A-pillar and round the headlights.

Extensive work was undertaken on the sill, bulkhead, door pillars and wheelarches. Good period secondhand doors also had to be found. Note: When buying secondhand doors they should be checked for rusting in the pockets. Also, replacement parts are available for the sliding window mechanism, runners and catches.

Replacement wings are easy to obtain and fairly inexpensive, but once again the labour element is likely to be the major part of the bill. The problems are usually caused by mud compacting round the back of the lights and at the top of the back of the wings.

The bonnet usually stays fairly good, although rust will form around the point where the grille surround is attached on Mk 2 and Mk 3 shells.

Subframes
While still outside the car, check both the subframes, particularly the rear one, which has not had the benefit of oil leaking on to it and preserving it. Also, inspect the floor beneath the rear seats and footwell, the battery box area, the petrol tank and the outer edges of the central crossmember,

particularly round the jacking points.

Inside the car
Inside the car you may find rot in the front footwell, under the passenger seat and where the wheelarches attach to the floorpan.

Having satisfied yourself as to the condition of the bodyshell, naturally, the interior trim must be looked at carefully, and here the major problems are likely to begin.

Trim for early Minis, the Wolseley and Riley and any Cooper is almost impossible to obtain. If you are not rebuilding a car with originality in mind, this may not cause you a problem, but it will if you want your car 'as original', and with classic car prices soaring daily for original cars, you should bear this in mind. You may well be OK with badges

The boot floor was also rusted and needed replacement. Note: The rear valance is only bolted to the car, the only panel attached in this way, but it is unlikely to be in good condition and will probably be extremely difficult to remove as the bolts will be very rusty.

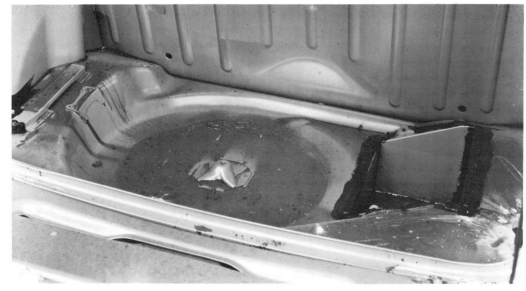

The boot is usually not only rusted in the spare wheel well, but often corroded by the battery, so it is as well to put some sealer round the battery bay.

On this car the floor was in reasonable condition, but beware, particularly on the Mk 1 bodyshells, which shipped water like camels; the floor is often very rusty and unsafe. It is also a wise precaution to change the loom which, as in this car, is often damaged by mice or insects – or simply rotted through. After trying all sorts of cleaners, the only way to clean the seats and door liners properly was to use cellulose thinners. The interior of this car was filthy, but came up almost like new after a good scrub with this unlikely cleaner.

When the underbonnet area was stripped, the master cylinders had looked beyond saving but were rescued with overhaul kits. All black items such as subframe and brackets were rubbed down and painted with Finnigan's Smoothrite.

and other parts, such as the Cooper speedo, which was unavailable for a number of years but is now being remanufactured.

Suspension

When buying your Mini check to see if the car is level, especially if it is one of the Hydrolastic-sprung cars, as a list can be symptomatic of further problems. In these cars, particularly the older ones, the pipes and pressure valves are at risk and may need replacing. Although this may be a bit costly on most of the models, it can be downright impossible on the Cooper S, for which Hydrolastic units are not currently available.

One good answer, if faced with a problem such as this, is to replace the whole of the suspension system with the dry-cone set-up, as originally and currently used.

If you are looking at a dry-cone car and still see sagging, and are satisfied that the problem is not rust, then it is most likely to be worn rubber cones or deteriorating trumpets and knuckles. These are simple to replace and relatively inexpensive. The trailing arms in the rear suspension may seize at their pivot points and in time they will wear a hole in the arm. Squeaking suspension is usually caused by the nylon seating of the trumpet having been worn through.

When looking at the car it is also useful to take a friend along who will be able to tell you whether the car is crabbing. If you detect this, check for accident damage.

On the front subframe, the main areas to look at are the cones, the rubber bearings in the upper arms, the rubber bushes on the lower arms and the swivel pins at the top and

The front subframe assembly showing the independent front suspension. This is the Hydrolastic version, which was not only more expensive to produce, but was also not particularly liked by the competition drivers. It was eventually substituted by the initial rubber suspension, which gives a choppy ride compared to more modern cars.

The rear radius arm fixing on the subframe is rarely as clean as this when you come to dismantle a car, so when it is being replaced it is as well to fit new corrosion-resistant nuts and bolts. When refitting new arms and trumpets into the subframe you may need a fair bit of patience or luck to do it quickly.

All bare metal was primed with red oxide followed by some good coats of primer filler to eliminate any minor pitting.

the bottom of the hubs. Otherwise, the main cause of problems will be damage, often caused by careless driving over obstacles such as kerbs.

Drivetrain

When driving the car, check for knocking noises from the front, particularly with the steering on full lock. This will indicate whether the constant velocity joints are on their way out. If you do hear knocks, the CV joints should be replaced – it is too risky to leave them to break up.

You should also listen for a similar sound on acceleration or deceleration, particularly on cars manufactured before May 1973, as this generally means that the rubber couplings on the drive-shafts are worn. These, too, should be replaced, as should the gaiters if they look as though they

have seen better days. Any dirt on the joints will accelerate wear and may have serious consequences.

Brakes

A poorly tended car is quite likely to have problems with its brakes, the most common sort being the seizing of the brake cylinders. Check the drums for grip, wear and rust, and likewise check the discs for wear as after many years' use they may be getting a bit thin.

Wheels and tyres

Check the tyres for uneven wear as this will indicate problems with the tracking. The wheels should be OK, although alloy ones may be corroded. If the car is still fitted with Denovo tyres – which is unlikely – then beware, as

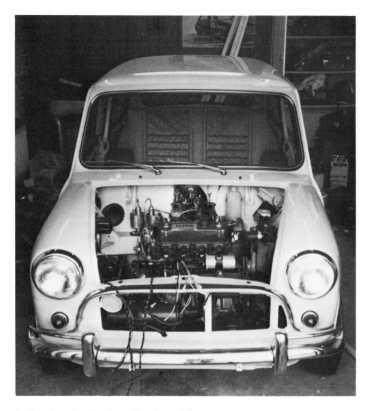

Following the final application of the top coat of paint, the first task was to install the engine, followed by retrimming the dash rails and windscreen pillars. Once all the glass had been fitted, all the box-sections were injected with polyurethane foam, just as BMC used to, to prevent leaks around the floorpan.

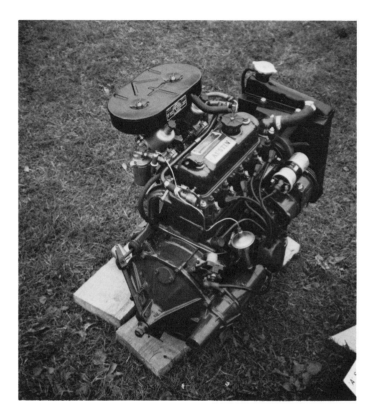

With hindsight, the engine should have been examined more carefully. Not being able to test it, Richard Mansfield found that it had a noisy bearing. The engine had to be removed later when it was found that one of the bearings had lost its brass cage. The whole unit was painstakingly painted with green Hermetite.

these tyres are fairly expensive and have a tendency to wear rather more rapidly than other types.

Mechanical aspects

The guideline most often given for the condition of an engine is the oil pressure. However, I believe this is unrealistic. For a start, only the Coopers are likely to be fitted with an oil pressure gauge – and if it is, is it working properly? However, if you do find one with the right instrument, the right pressure for a standard car at idle speed is around 15psi, increasing to about 40psi during driving. The bigger-engined and quicker cars are different; the 1275GT should show around 60psi while the Cooper S engines rate even higher at 75psi. In most cases a variation of up to 40% does not mean that the engine is about to disintegrate, but rather that it may require attention.

You must listen to the engine and decide whether it is running smoothly and if there is excessive timing chain rattle. Often, a better test than the psi reading for the amateur is to take along a compression tester – obtainable fairly cheaply from Halfords or your local motor factor. The key here is that the pressures should be similar, although not too low, as this will indicate loose or worn piston rings.

Look at the engine, particularly down the back of the block, where you may find oil leaks. If these are low down on the block, they may be more serious than you initially thought, as it could mean removing the engine, splitting it and reassembling. If the car is a standard one, you may feel it is hardly worth the bother of an engine rebuild and go instead for a reconditioned unit.

Gearbox

While driving, feel for evidence of a sloppy gearchange and

The worst job, the complete overhaul of the suspension system and brakes, was left until last. For safety reasons nothing was left to chance and practically everything was renewed, including of course all the operating brake parts. All the renovated parts were painted with Finnigan's Smoothrite.

watch out for the gear-lever slipping out of gear. Check the mounting points, particularly the bracket on the differential casing, as this is a well-known point.

Listen out for excessive gear whine as this could lead to a damaged gearbox casing. Of course, synchromesh does wear, mostly on the second gear. As you might expect, the later boxes are cheaper to replace, but if you have problems with your earlier box, particularly a Cooper close-ratio one, you should repair it rather than exchange it.

Clutch slip should only be evident on early cars, unless the clutch is completely worn. If the clutch is fairly new, the problem is likely to be oil leaking through the oil seal. It will need removal of the engine, although some people claim to be able to change a clutch in situ on earlier cars.

Which car have I bought?
The most sought-after cars are the Coopers and therefore they are the ones most likely to be faked. There is no harm in this as long as the converter does not try to sell the car as

The original blue carpets are no longer available through the Rover Group, so Richard Mansfield contacted his local carpet shop, who were able to supply material which was a perfect match in both colour and texture.

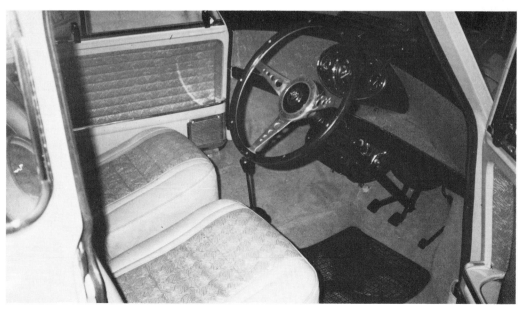

Although the seat material cleaned up perfectly with cellulose thinners, there still remained the task of repainting the silver inlay on the brocade material. This took some 25 hours to complete using a very fine-tipped Pilot pen – and a steady hand!

The original grille was missing from the car and one was obtained following a chance meeting with someone in MiniSpares, at Friern Barnet, North London. He had a brand new grille, still in its box, for £30. What luck! Other items like overriders, corner bars and door handles were obtained secondhand and rechromed, and the restoration was complete.

an original one.

Refer to the Mini-Cooper and Mini-Cooper S identification guide in Chapter 3 to check authenticity.

One system given for checking the age of the car is to look at the date stamp on the windscreen wiper motor – unless, of course, it has been changed, in which case you may have to resort to checking whether all the windows have the same coding.

CHAPTER 8

The Mini specials

Specialist sports derivatives

Once the Mini was on the market it didn't take long for people to catch on to the idea that their plain appearance could be embellished or that because of their subframe construction it would be no problem to use the Mini mechanicals as a basis for a complete redesign.

Initially the craze was started off by 'goon' Peter Sellers in 1961 when he decided he would like wickerwork on his door panels. The work was done by Hooper, the Rolls-Royce people, via H R Owen. Although this customized Mini caused a sensation, Hooper didn't want to know, although one Harold Radford did. Up to this time he had been making and fitting walnut items, such as cocktail cabinets, to Rolls-Royces, but he decided that the Mini presented a greater chance for his business.

His company, which was soon taken over by H R Owen, started producing luxury Minis on a production line, but when the demand dried up they couldn't make ends meet and eventually disappeared. In the meantime, they had also produced a Mini with a tailgate for Peter Sellers – the first of many such conversions.

Meanwhile, two of Hooper's employees, Bill Wood and Les Pickett, had left to form their own company, which became even more famous for its Mini conversions and is still in business today. Instead of producing vehicles and hoping to sell them, their policy was always to build to order only, and in this way they survived the lean years.

Harold Radford's first Mini, revealed in the latter half of 1963, cost £1,100 when a standard car was just £500 and had a level of comfort never imagined possible in such a basic car; it was everything that Issigonis had not envisaged for his car. There was a radio (an instrument which Issigonis thought simply distracted the driver), a rear demister, electric windows, a sun roof, white leather seats and thick pile carpets, and a redesigned binnacle with the instruments set in front of the driver.

The only problem was that with all this extra stuff inside the car it had the performance of a rice pudding, so Downton was called in to tune the engine and match the performance to the luxury.

The luxury continued to rise and eventually there was foam, underfelt and thicker pile carpets so that the interior became like a cocoon, with even the engine noise almost completely blocked out.

The Cooper Car Company also saw the opportunity and in 1966 commissioned Bertone to bring the Mini up-market. Their approach was a lot more understated, with a less flashy interior styling, but concentrating on re-upholstering and shaping of seats to provide more lateral support, as is more common in motor sport. The inside of the doors was also given the treatment with the addition of electric windows and quarter-lights.

Then Arab oil money came to Britain, which pushed the cost of one or two Minis up to the £¼ million mark. But these had everything from colour televisions and telephones to air conditioning and quadrophonic music centres – plus, of course, even more powerful engines, just to shift the additional weight.

While all this serious conversion was going on, there was

The craze for embellishing the Mini was started when Peter Sellers asked H R Owen to put wickerwork panels on the doors of his car. Naturally, BMC had to see what they could come up with, and this was the result. This car included a full-length sunroof, headlamp cowlings and over-the-top hub caps.

also the not-so-serious, and through the years there has been the longest Mini, the shortest Mini, the lowest Mini, the tallest Mini, an orange-shaped Mini, and there was even a scheme at one time to use private Minis as advertising hoardings. Owners could rent their space to an advertising company, which would respray their car with the appropriate company's name, logo and design in return for money. Many owners took up the opportunity as at the end of the contracted period their car was given a free respray.

With the exception of Ogle, who did a coupe early on in the Mini's career, it took a little time for the specialist versions to begin to appear. Of course today the Mini is probably the most widely used base for kit cars of all shapes and sizes from Mini concept copies to Mini Lamborghinis. Other companies which made good use of Mini components were Marcos, Unipower, Minipower, GTM, Crayford and Broadspeed.

The Mini Marcos was one of the most widely known of the Mini specials as it was highly successful for a short period of time. Launched in 1965, it was popular for racing

and amazingly enough proved itself suitable for racing at Le Mans, being the only British finisher in the 1966 race.

In 1967 Mini-Marcos was sold to D&H Fibreglass Techniques of Oldham, which was run by Harold Dermott, a former Jaguar development engineer. Production of the Mini-Marcos continued until 1981, although a new model, called the Midas, was unveiled in 1978. The new car was a 2+2 glassfibre monocoque and was generally regarded as an extremely successful design. One well known proponent of the car is Gordon Murray, the Formula 1 race car designer.

The Unipower was one of the best produced of all the early Mini derivatives – and the price of the kit of around £1,200 with Cooper S engine in 1967 reflected that. It was mid-engined, extremely light and very quick.

The Unipower was designed by Val Dare-Bryan and Ernest Unger in 1963 and the prototype was completed in the workshop of the racing driver Roy Pierpoint. The project was taken over by Tim Powell, who ran Universal Power Drives, the makers of Unipower tractor units. Although the prototype had an aluminium body the production vehicles

For a while there was an advertising gimmick in 1977 in which Mini owners rented out the space on their car to be used as an advertising hoarding for a set period.

The subframe construction of the car meant that it was ideal for the special builder. This vehicle is using a Cooper S engine and Hydrolastic suspension.

The special 1,275cc Mini Traveller introduced at the 1967 Racing Car Show by the Cooper Car Company. The equipment level was lavish and included rectangular headlamps, sidelights and spotlights, special paint, Cooper magnesium wheels, reclining seats, a fully-equipped facia and leather seats and steering wheel.

The comprehensively equipped interior of the 1,275cc Mini Traveller from the Cooper Car Company. Not only a different dash with map light, but also leather seats and steering wheel and thick pile carpets.

This publicity stunt was well put together. It is in fact two Minis joined by a metal bridge and depicting three famous rally cars with a piece of metal bridging them. The inner wheels are concealed by the plate in the middle. The rally plates refer to no.144 in the 1967 Monte driven by Makinen, no.82 driven in the Acropolis Rally by Makinen in 1966, and no.47 in the Marathon de la Route was the John Handley entry in the 1970 event.

Mini on Mini. Obviously, with the subframe construction of the Mini, this sort of vehicle is fairly simple to construct. This is Mike Chaplin, who built the six-wheel truck and could often be seen at shows with it carrying his customized saloon.

The elegant Unipower, one of the most successful designs for a small sports car based on Mini mechanicals. The prototype had aluminium panels, but the production model which first appeared in 1966 had a glassfibre bodyshell.

The Mini Marcos was probably the most successful in terms of sales of all the Mini-based sports cars. Superseded by the Midas, it was originally a little brother to the bigger Marcos sports cars.

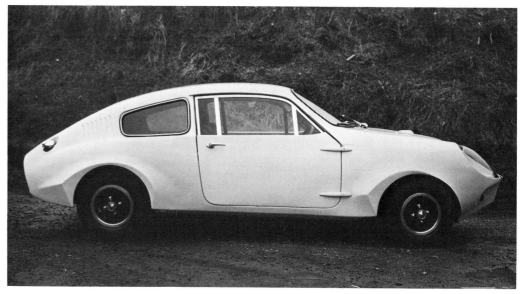

Not a Mercedes experimental car for a small saloon, but the whim of an individual who obviously liked the Mercedes look and the Mini comfort level! The German company was not amused.

which appeared at the 1966 London Racing Car Show had glassfibre bodies – but retained the Mini running gear. The total number of cars built is 75, of which half were exported.

The Minipower, designed and built by Brian Luff, was a rear-engined sports car which had little appeal; only 20 were ever completed.

Longer-lived than most, the GTM was popular. It had a semi-monocoque steel box chassis, with modified Mini front subframes attached at both front and rear. Introduced at the 1967 London Racing Car Show, it has survived, with more than 100 examples being completed.

Crayford were one of the companies that found the Mini was a good source of income, building convertibles and one-offs, with emphasis on the trim. Although the company has now changed hands, it was one of the few firms which survived from the early days of the Mini to today. Since Crayford started the craze, there have been numerous copies of their convertible. A Landaulette version (called the Mini Skirt) is now available from the Oxted Trimming Company, and is of considerably higher standard than most.

Designers have found it difficult over the years to build styling kits that don't make the Mini look grotesque, too wide or too chunky. This Kat kit just about manages to look OK, although the tyres are far too fat.

CHAPTER 9

Recent history

1275 GT and later developments

The first few years of Mini production were hectic, with the factory having little chance of putting into volume production the lessons they were learning from their competition experience. Naturally there were some changes, but they were only introduced if they were deemed vital.

The complete Mini range was rationalized in October 1967 when it was standardized into the basic saloon, which used the 848cc engine, and the Super de Luxe 1000 models, which used the 998cc engine. The estate cars, the Riley Elf and Wolseley Hornet were fitted with the larger engine, while the commercial vehicles and the Mini Moke, which had been introduced in August 1964, used the smaller unit. However, the larger engine was an option on the commercials such as the Pick-up and the Van.

By this time, too, the bigger-engined models had the Cooper remote-type gear-lever, rather than the long stick type of lever.

The introduction of seat belts caused some problems, mostly because humans weren't built with gorilla-length arms. This had the effect of preventing them getting at the switch gear if they were sensibly strapped in. Now, of course, we have inertia-reel belts, but they were not available at first, so when the Mk2 shell was introduced the switch gear was moved 3in nearer the driver. Inertia-reel belts were finally introduced as standard in February 1974.

The Mk2 shell also saw the new wider rear window – an inch wider on each side – additional interior trim, along with better seats, and a larger front grille.

Other improvements were a turning circle reduced from 32ft to 28ft – achieved by increasing the number of teeth on the rack from 15 to 25 and increasing the length of the steering arms by just 0.094in.

A number of niceties, which many thought took the character out of the Mini, were introduced with the Mk2 shell, the most noticeable being the deletion of the floor-mounted dipswitch (the floor-mounted starter button had disappeared in September 1961). The dipswitch was taken into the stalk, which now also contained the indicators and horn push. The winking indicator light was also taken off the stalk and put into the binnacle and, wonder of wonders, self-parking windscreen wipers were fitted. The cable door release was replaced in June 1968 by a proper handle.

Next to come were the all-synchromesh gearboxes throughout the range by September 1968. The Mk2 models were replaced with another shell, Mk 3, codenamed ADO 20, offering wind-up windows, concealed door hinges and a reversion to dry-cone suspension from the Hydrolastic type, which had been introduced in September 1964.

Then there was the Mini Clubman – a study in how not to improve the design of a car. It was 4in longer, had a flatter nose, slightly inferior performance to the original Minis of the same specification, and only of any benefit to the mechanics who valued the extra space under the bonnet. Nevertheless, Austin Morris' sales director, Filmer Paradise, used to quote market research that showed that some people felt safer in longer-nosed cars!

The Clubman was introduced with the 998cc engine, Hydrolastic suspension – it had been discontinued for the

There were many attempts by the British Leyland management to redesign the Mini. This one code-named ADO 70 is a Michelotti prototype, which uses the Mini 1275 GT mechanicals and was considered in 1970 as a replacement for the MG Midget in the USA.

ADO 34, an earlier prototype styled by Pininfarina in Italy and fitted with the Mini-Cooper S engine.

The Innocenti Mini was produced in Italy and perhaps reflected the way the Mini might easily have gone in the UK if there had been a more imaginative management. It used basically the same mechanicals, but in an admirably updated hatchback body design. Designed by Bertone, the body continues as the Innocenti 900 but with a Daihatsu engine.

The Mini Mayfair has been in continuous production since 1982 and is the more luxuriously equipped of the two-model basic range. The other entry-level car is the Mini City, and both use the 998cc engine, the 848cc unit having been discontinued in 1979.

The Mini Mayfair interior. Although it is still recognizably a Mini, the instruments have been moved in front of the driver and air vents are standard.

standard cars – and improved seats, trim and instrumentation, which was now directly in front of the driver rather than in the centre of the dash area.

After Donald Stokes had taken over and the Cooper range was dropped, thus depriving John Cooper of the princely sum of £2 a car (total Cooper and Cooper S production was 144,910), the 1275GT, using the Clubman bodyshell, was introduced. Designed to be a replacement for the Coopers and to help bring the insurance group of the top-end vehicle down, it was a complete failure in those terms, but as a car in its own right it can be counted a success.

The engine retained the bore and stroke dimensions of the Cooper S, but it was in fact the unit which was being used in the 1300 range of cars. It produced a lot less power, just 59bhp compared with 76bhp for the 1275 Cooper S, but it had the edge in torque with 84lb/ft compared with 79lb/ft. It also had a lower compression ratio at 8.3:1 compared with 9.75:1. It lacked the excitement of the S version and was difficult to uprate, having a different head and bottom end. To try and compensate for the lack of power, the final-drive ratio was lowered to 3.44:1 from 3.65:1, but this experiment only lasted a year – presumably considered to be the length of time taken by the public to forget about the Cooper ancestry.

In fact there was a period when both Cooper S and 1275GT were produced side-by-side, but this didn't last long and was simply a heavy-handed attempt to subtly phase-out the Cooper.

In March 1970, the 1275 Cooper S was 'Clubmanized' with the introduction of what is called the Mk3 or ADO 20 shell, which included hidden door hinges, Clubman trim and wind-up windows. In July 1971, the last Cooper S rolled off the production line... a sad event.

Meanwhile, change was running on apace with alternators being fitted as standard in December 1972, along with improved synchromesh. In April 1973, a new rod gearchange was introduced, inertia seat belts were fitted as standard in February 1974, and 1974 also saw the option of laminated windscreens and Denovo tyres. In July 1974, the petrol tank on the 1275GT was enlarged by 2 gallons – no need now for the twin tanks.

In the winter of 1973/74 the UK was deep in an oil crisis and though the Mini should realistically have been at the end of its natural life, it suddenly became popular again. While the development teams were working away at the Mini replacement, coded ADO 88, options continued to be offered for the Mini. A 1,098cc engine, as used in the 1100 series, was now fitted from October 1974 in the Clubman, and BL began to awaken to the Special Edition market.

By 1976, ADO 88 was just about ready and required only the green light. It was slightly wider – by 2in – quieter and the ride was improved, and of course it was a different design. It turned out to be just the latest in a long line of redesign efforts, although it was the one that came closest to replacing the Mini altogether.

With Michael Edwardes in place as company boss, taking over from Alex Park in November 1977, the resources were channelled into the production of the LC8 – later to be the Metro – and it was not until the introduction of the Metro in 1980 that the Mini received any substantial attention.

The Mini Sprite, adopting the name of another famous BMC sporting car, was typical of the special edition syndrome, with very little extra to offer apart from stripes, black bumpers and minor changes in the interior.

Then it was given a version of the new A-Plus engine, which had a stiffer block wall for quietness, a crankshaft torsional damper, a longer-lasting crankshaft and other important changes, along with a redesigned transmission.

To prevent the car going too up-market, the Mini City was introduced, which offered another generation of drivers the central speedometer, although with greater comfort in the ordinary Mini shell. Then there were the economical 1000HLE and City E models in April 1982, which coincided with the phasing-out of the estate bodyshells.

Slowly the basic models began to creep up the luxury scale in the UK and soon the Mayfair was replacing the 1000HLE, and the City E was getting reversing lights and passenger sun visors, plus the heated rear windscreen.

Perhaps the most noticeable change was the adoption of 12in wheels throughout the range in 1984, which didn't just have a visual impact but also provided plenty of room for front discs. The 1275GT had been fitted with these wheels and disc brakes since 1974.

Today's Mini
Since then the Mini has become a series of Special Editions, starting with the Mini Sprite, the Mini Chelsea, the Mini Ritz and continuing with the Mini Park Lane, the Mini 25, the Jet Black, the Red Hot, and for 1989, the Flame, Racing, Sky and Rose models. Although the Mini enthusiast may mourn the passing of the genuinely sporting versions, there is one last fling with a 115mph ERA version, which, although not officially a Rover Group product, has been given their blessing. This is in addition to the leather-trimmed Mini Thirty, released by Rover to mark the car's 30th birthday.

The new Cooper
With the re-awakening of interest in the Mini in its 30th year, the Cooper badge is to be seen once again on the car –

A selection of the special edition models for the Mini's 30th year. The white tops of the two nearest cars reflect the Coopers of the 1960s, although in performance 'Flame' and 'Racing' are nowhere near as quick.

The first and the latest. 621 AOK was the first hand-built car ever produced and is still in the possession of the Rover Group. The car on the left is the special edition Mini Thirty.

although, alas, it isn't the Rover Group which is producing it, but John Cooper himself.

The 1989 Cooper is a kit, fitted by John Cooper Garages at Ferring, near Worthing in West Sussex, and is designed to pep up the current factory offerings to bring back the spirit of the original Mini-Coopers, if not their actual performance.

The kit comprises a balanced, polished and gas-flowed cylinder head with larger inlet and exhaust valves, which is designed to run on 95 octane unleaded fuel.

As with the Coopers, twin 1.25in SU carburettors are fitted on a polished inlet manifold, complete with K & N air filters. There is a new three-branch exhaust manifold and exhaust system. All this raises the power output from the current standard 43bhp to 64bhp, allowing the retention of the standard suspension and brakes.

On the cosmetic side, there is the traditional Cooper grille and an alloy rocker cover, plus Karmono Mistral alloy wheels.

Performance is considerably better than your average Mini with a 0–60mph time of 13.2 seconds. Not superfast, you might think, but then the Rover Group has changed the diff ratio to 3.1 from the 3.7, which gave considerably better acceleration. If you want to improve performance, a change is possible, though be warned, the 3.7 diff is difficult to find these days and you may have to be satisfied with a 3.4 diff which is available off the shelf.

The Cooper Mini is capable of 88mph from an engine producing 64bhp at 6,000rpm. The cost of the conversion in summer 1989 was £1,466.25, including the new wheels. The extras are a Moto Lita steering wheel, overriders and Cooper badges.

A new ERA
The ERA car is another proposition altogether. Perhaps not the prettiest Mini around, it is nevertheless going to go down in history as the fastest production model. Rumour has it that testing speeds approaching 130mph prompted the fitting of a wastegate restrictor limiting the maximum speed to 115mph for safety reasons.

The very full engine bay of the turbocharged ERA Mini, which has a top speed of around 115mph. The brick-like design of the Mini restricts the top speed, although it was rumoured that in testing this car proved capable of 135mph before the output was restricted to a speed more appropriate for a production vehicle of this size.

Each car is hand-built by ERA at Dunstable. The company's origins are in English Racing Automobiles, which did so much to keep Britain's name high in motor racing immediately before and after World War 2, but it is now called Engineering Research and Application and is more usually involved in fuel systems research and engine certification.

With the agreement and co-operation of Rover, who offer the car through their dealers, ERA take a Mini City bodyshell and squeeze in the engine and transmission from the MG Metro Turbo. This involves some fairly extensive bodywork modifications as well as changes to the lubrication and cooling systems and corresponding up-rating of suspension and brakes. The latter have ventilated front discs with four-pot calipers; 13in wheels are fitted and accommodated beneath wheelarches which form part of the outer body modifications.

The manufacturer's claimed 0–60mph acceleration time of 7.8sec is quick but not perhaps what one might expect from a light car with 94bhp at the wheels. However, it really comes into its own in the mid-range, with a 30–50mph time in 2nd gear of 3.4sec and 50–70 in 3rd gear in 6.3sec.

ERA see the Mini Turbo as the 1980s equivalent of the Mini-Cooper S, offering 'speed, handling and excitement'

The full leather interior of the ERA Mini, which retails for around £12,000. Perhaps not quite the car that Issigonis intended, and quite a toy for the people who can afford it. Designed as the Cooper of the 1990s, it has a limited production life of two years.

while introducing the refinement and comfort lacking in the original car.

As well as being the fastest-ever volume production Mini – by some distance – this is also the most expensive, costing £11,500 when launched in mid-1989. An unofficial performance special, the M-30 from the British Automobile Company of North Perrott, Somerset, was launched at the August 1989 Mini celebration at Silverstone. It also uses a 1,300cc MG Metro engine, but with a Sprintex mechanical supercharger, so that it develops 115bhp. Elaborately trimmed and equipped, it costs no less than £30,000!

These exotic versions aside, in its 30th year the Mini is back to the people's car that Issigonis intended – small, economical, good handling, and fun to drive. Total Mini production in 1989 remained a healthy 40,000. Britain remained the best market, but Japan had overtaken France as the best area for export sales.

An even more elaborate Mini special built to celebrate the 30th anniversary is the BAC M-30, produced by the British Automobile Company. Bodywork modifications are based on Simon Saunders' KAT design but 1.3 litre engine is thoroughly re-worked with a Sprintex supercharger and output increased to 115bhp. BAC set out to make just 30 examples, at £30,000 each.

APPENDIX A

Technical specifications

Every Mini uses a version of the BMC A-Series engine, which has four cylinders, in-line, and is mounted transversely in the car, with the gearbox underslung. The engine uses a cast-iron cylinder head and a cast-iron block, which on the earlier engines carried two tappet chest covers on the side of the block. All heads contain two valves per cylinder, in-line, which are operated by pushrods and rockers from the camshaft mounted in the side of the block on the rearward facing side.

The body is constructed of pressed sheet steel panels, built as a box unit with front and rear subframes for the suspension.

Basic data is as follows; variations are noted under individual model headings.

Overall length: 10ft 0.25in
Width: 4ft 7.5in
Height: 4ft 5in
Wheelbase: 6ft 8in
Front track: 3ft 11.75in
Rear track: 3ft 9.875in
Tyres and wheels: 10in x 3.5in
Front suspension: Transverse wishbones with Moulton rubber cone and tie rod
Rear suspension: Trailing arm and Moulton rubber cone
Steering: Rack and pinion

Austin Seven and Morris Mini-Minor (Later called Austin and Morris Mini, then just Mini)

Introduced: August 1959
Ceased production: 1980
Engine: Type 8MB
Capacity: 848cc
Bore: 62.94mm
Stroke: 68.26mm
Compression ratio: 8.3:1
Max power: 34bhp at 5,500rpm, later 37bhp (33 DIN) at 5,250rpm
Max torque: 44lb/ft at 2,900rpm, later at 2,500rpm
Gear ratios: 1st, 13.658:1; 2nd, 8.177:1; 3rd, 5.316:1; 4th, 3.765:1
Final drive: 3.765:1
Brakes: 7in drums front and rear

Austin Mini-Cooper, Morris Mini-Cooper 997

Introduced: October 1961
Ceased production: December 1963
Engine: Type 9F
Capacity: 997cc
Bore: 62.43mm
Stroke: 81.28mm

Compression ratio: 9:1 (8.3:1 optional)
Valve sizes: Inlet, 29.4mm; exhaust 25.4mm; lift 7.29mm
Max power: 55bhp at 6,000rpm
Max torque: 54lb/ft at 3,600rpm
Carburation: Twin SU HS2, 31.75mm choke diameter. Two wire air cleaners
Gear ratios: Std: 12.05, 7.213, 5.11, 3.765:1. Option: 11.01, 6.598, 4.674, 3.765:1.
Final drive: 3.765:1 (3.44 option)
Brakes: Front: 7in discs. Rear: 7in drums x 1.25in wide.

Austin Mini-Cooper, Morris Mini-Cooper 998

Introduced: January 1964
Ceased production: November 1969
Engine: Type 9FA
Capacity: 998cc
Bore: 64.588mm
Stroke: 76.20mm
Compression ratio: 9:1 (7.8:1 optional)
Valve sizes: Inlet, 30.86mm; exhaust 25.4mm; lift 7.29mm
Max power: 55bhp at 5,800rpm
Max torque: 57lb/ft at 3,000rpm
Carburation: Twin SU HS2, 31.75mm choke diameter. Two wire air cleaners
Gear ratios: Std: 12.05, 7.213, 5.11, 3.765:1. Option: 11.01, 6.598, 4.674, 3.44:1.
Final drive: 3.765:1 (3.44 option)
Brakes: Front: 7in discs. Rear: 7in drums x 1.25in wide

Mini-Cooper

Notes on model changes

March 1963	Brakes improved from chassis L/A257 313830 (rhd) and C/A257L212740 (lhd)
January 1964	998cc Cooper introduced
February 1964	Windscreen wiper arc reduced to avoid fouling screen surround
March 1964	Dunlop SP41 radials fitted
July 1964	Rear brakes get lower anti-lock pressure settings
September 1964	Hydrolastic suspension fitted. From engine 9FD SAH1701, new gearchange forks with larger contact area fitted Diaphragm spring clutch fitted from engine 9FS SAH3780
October 1964	Improved driveshaft couplings
November 1964	Driver's seat gets three-position setting
January 1965	Better radiator fitted – 16 grilles per inch
May 1965	Primary gears get scroll-type oil seal from engines 9FD SAH6448 and 9FD SAL935
January 1966	Leading edge of exterior handles gets safety boss
October 1967	Plastic fan fitted Mk2 bodyshell introduced with larger rear window and rear lamps and Super de-luxe trim
September 1968	All-synchro gearbox introduced

Mini-Cooper S 1071

Introduced: March 1963
Discontinued: August 1964
Capacity: 1,071cc
Bore: 70.60mm
Stroke: 68.26mm
Compression ratio: 9:1
Valve sizes: Inlet, 35.71mm; exhaust 30.96mm; lift 7.29mm
Max power: 70bhp at 6,000rpm
Max torque: 62lb/ft at 4,500rpm
Carburation: Twin SU HS2, 31.75mm choke diameter. Two wire air cleaners.
Gear ratios: Std: 12.05, 7.213, 5.11, 3.765:1. Option: 11.01, 6.598, 4.674, 3.44:1.
Final drive: 3.765:1 (3.44 option)
Brakes: Front: 7.5in discs. Rear: 7in drums x 1.25ins wide.
Front track: 4ft 0.58in
Rear track: 3ft 11.3in
Wheels: 10 x 4.5in

Mini-Cooper S 970

Introduced: September 1964
Discontinued: January 1965
Capacity: 970cc
Bore: 70.60mm
Stroke: 61.91mm
Compression ratio: 9.75:1
Valve sizes: Inlet, 35.71mm; exhaust 30.96mm; lift 7.29mm
Max power: 65bhp at 6,500rpm
Max torque: 55lb/ft at 3.500rpm
Carburation: Twin SU HS2, 31.75mm choke diameter. Two wire air cleaners.
Gear ratios: Std: 12.05, 7.213, 5.11, 3.765:1 Option: 11.01, 6.598, 4.674, 3.44:1.
Final drive: 3.765:1 (3.44 option)
Brakes: Front: 7.5in discs. Rear: 7in drums x 1.25in wide.
Front track: 4ft 0.58in
Rear track: 3ft 11.3in
Wheels: 10 x 4.5in

Mini-Cooper S 1275

Introduced: September 1964
Discontinued: July 1971
Capacity: 1,275cc
Bore: 70.60mm
Stroke: 81.33mm
Compression ratio: 9.5:1
Valve sizes: Inlet, 35.71mm; exhaust 30.96mm; lift 7.29mm
Max power: 76bhp at 5,800rpm
Max torque: 79lb/ft at 3,000rpm
Carburation: Twin SU HS2, 31.75mm choke diameter. Two wire air cleaners.
Gear ratios: Std: 12.05, 7.213, 5.11, 3.765:1. Option: 11.01, 6.598, 4.674, 3.44:1.
Final drive: 3.765:1 (3.44 option)
Brakes: Front: 7.5in discs. Rear: 7in drums x 1.25in wide.
Front track: 4ft 0.58in
Rear track: 3ft 11.3in

Mini-Cooper S

Notes on model changes

February 1964	Windscreen wiper arc reduced to avoid fouling windscreen surround
July 1964	Rear brakes get lower anti-lock pressure setting
September 1964	Hydrolastic suspension fitted Diaphragm spring clutch fitted from engines: 9F SAX29001 (970cc), 9F SAH33260 (1,071cc), and 9F SAY31001 (1,275cc) Positive crankcase ventilation from engines: 9FD SAX29004 (970cc), and 9FD SAY31406 (1,275cc)
November 1964	Driver's seat gets three-position setting
January 1965	970S car discontinued. Only 1,275cc version of S-type remains in production
January 1966	Twin petrol tanks fitted as standard. Oil cooler fitted as standard
April/May 1966	Higher rate Hydrolastic units, new steel and rubber lower wishbone bush, plus rear hub bearings get roller bearing. Also inboard end of driveshaft gets solid universal joint. Suspension mountings strengthened from chassis C/A 257 851199 (Austin), and K/A 254 851028 (Morris)
October 1967	Mk2 bodyshell introduced with larger rear window and Super de-Luxe trim Gradual fit of all-synchro gearbox started
March 1970	Mk3 bodyshell introduced with wind-up windows, and Clubman trim, seats, and doors (including concealed hinges).
October 1970	Ignition shield, from car N20 D528A

Mini Clubman

Introduced: October 1969
Discontinued: 1980
Body: Mini Clubman
Length: 11ft 1.875in
Capacity: 998cc
Bore: 64.588mm
Stroke: 76.2mm
Compression ratio: 8.3:1
Max power: 38bhp at 5,250rpm
Max torque: 52lb/ft at 2,700rpm
Gear ratios: 13.657, 8.176, 5.317, 3.765:1

Mini 1275GT

Introduced: October 1969
Discontinued: 1980
Body: Mini Clubman
Length: 11ft 1.875in
Engine type: 12H
Capacity: 1,275cc
Bore: 70.64mm
Stroke: 81.28mm
Compression ratio: 8.8:1
Valve sizes: Inlet, 35.71mm; exhaust 30.96mm; lift 7.29mm
Max power: 59bhp at 5,300rpm
Max torque: 65lb/ft at 2,550rpm
Carburation: Twin SU HS2, 31.75mm choke diameter. Two wire air cleaners.
Gear ratios: Std: 12.87, 8.10, 5.22, 3.65:1. Later: 12.13, 7.63, 4.92, 3.44:1.
Final drive: 3.65:1. To 3.44:1 in December 1970
Brakes: Front: 7.5in discs. Rear: 7in drums x 1.25in wide.
Front track: 4ft 0.58in
Rear track: 3ft 11.3in
Wheels and tyres: 4.5in. 12in x 4.5in from 1974

Note on model changes: Hydrolastic suspension originally but dry cone suspension fitted from June 1971

Mini Clubman 1100

Introduced: October 1975
Discontinued: 1980
Body: Mini Clubman
Length: 11ft 1.875in
Engine type: 10
Capacity: 1,098cc
Bore: 64.588mm
Stroke: 83.7mm
Compression ratio: 8.5:1
Max power: 45bhp at 5,000rpm
Max torque: 56lb/ft at 2,700rpm
Gear ratios: 13.657, 8.176, 5.317, 3.765:1

Mini 1.0E Mayfair

Specification as in 1989:
Length: 10ft 1in
Engine type: A-Plus
Capacity: 998cc
Bore: 64.58mm
Stroke: 76.20mm
Compression ratio: 10.3:1
Valve sizes: Inlet, 28.80mm; exhaust 25.45mm; lift 7.24mm
Max power: 40bhp at 5,000rpm
Max torque: 50lb/ft at 2,500rpm
Carburation: SU HS4
Gear ratios: Std: 13.73, 8.23, 5.76, 3.765:1
Final drive: 3.765:1
Brakes: Front: 8.4in discs. Rear: 7in drums x 1.25in wide
Front track: 4ft 0.58in
Rear track: 3ft 11.3in
Wheels and tyres: 4.5in, 12in x 4.5in
Kerb weight: 1,420lb

APPENDIX D

Useful addresses

Clubs

Mini-Cooper Club – Joyce Holman, 1 Weavers Cottages, Church Hill, West Hoathly, West Sussex. Tel: 0342 8100662

Mini-Cooper Register – Carol Evans, 394 Gressal Lane, Tile Cross, Birmingham. Tel: 021 779 5183

Mini Moke Club – Paul Beard, 13 Ashdene Close, Hartlebury, Worcs. DY11 7TN. Tel: 0299 250756

Mini Owners' Club – 15 Birchwood Road, Lichfield, Staffs. WS14 9UN

Mini Seven Racing Club – Mrs K A Tisdale, 33 Stoke Road, Slough, Berks. SL2 5AH

Suppliers

Bumper to Bumper, 38 London Road, Kessingland, Nr Lowestoft, Suffolk. Tel: 0502 740128. Trim, body panels and mechanical items.

John Cooper Cars, 50 Ferring Street, Ferring, Worthing, West Sussex. BN12 5JP. Tel: 0903 504455 The home of John Cooper. Some original style interior trim, Cooper insignia and original fittings.

DD Automotive Services, Unit 3 Churchill Buildings, Churchill Road, Doncaster. DN1 2TF. Tel: 0302 341153. Mail order parts.

Discount Mini Centre, New Road, Rainham, Essex. RN13 8SH. Tel: 0402 758048. Most parts new and secondhand.

Janspeed Engineering Ltd, Castle Road, Salisbury, Wilts. SP1 3SQ. Tel: 0722 21833. One of the original Mini specialists and tuners. Exhaust specialist, plus performance parts.

Mainly Minis, Lodge Farm, Lower South Park Road, South Godstone, Surrey. RH9 8LE. Tel: 0342 893191. Servicing, restoration and new and secondhand spares.

Minimail, Dymock, Gloucestershire. Tel: 053185 325. Mail order specialists.

Mini Spares Centre Ltd, 29–31 Friern Barnet Road, Southgate, London. N11 1NE. Tel: 01-368 6292. BMIHT-approved Mini specialist. Largest stock of parts in the UK, original and remanufactured.

Mini Sprint, 295 Avenue Road Extension, off Welford Road, Leics. Tel: 0533 702996. Restoration specialists and parts suppliers. Engine and gearbox modifications.

Oxford Engine Services (Oselli), Ferry Hinksey Road, Osney, Oxford. OX2 0BY. Tel: 0865 248100. BMIHT-approved engine specialists, and a leading tuning company.

Westford Mini and Metro Centre, 4 Bath Place West, The Octagon, Plymouth, Devon. Tel: 0752 665205. Restoration specialists and tuners.